WEIRDEST WAR TWO

WEIRDEST WAR TWO

RICHARD DENHAM

&

M. J. TROW

Copyright © 2021 Richard Denham & M. J. Trow.

www.blkdogpublishing.com

Other titles by Richard Denham

The Britannia Trilogy

World of Britannia: Historical Companion to the Britannia Trilogy

Arthur: Shadow of a God

Robin Hood: English Outlaw

Prester John: Africa's Lost King

Other titles by M. J. Trow

The Maxwell Series

The Inspector Lestrade Series

The Children's Crusade

Richard III in the North

The Killer of the Princes in the Tower

Other titles in the *Weird War Two* series

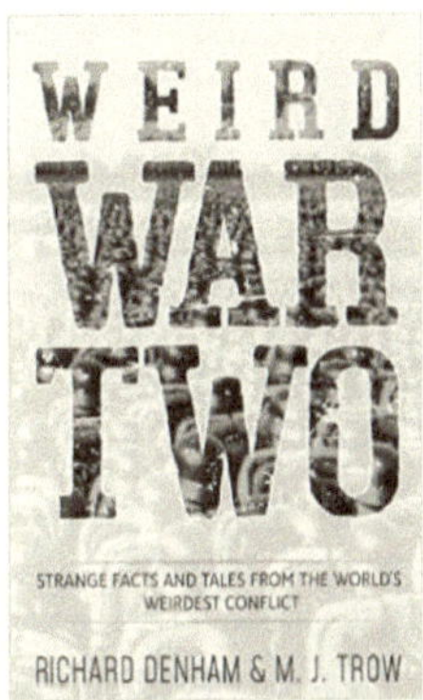

Weird War Two by Richard Denham & M. J. Trow

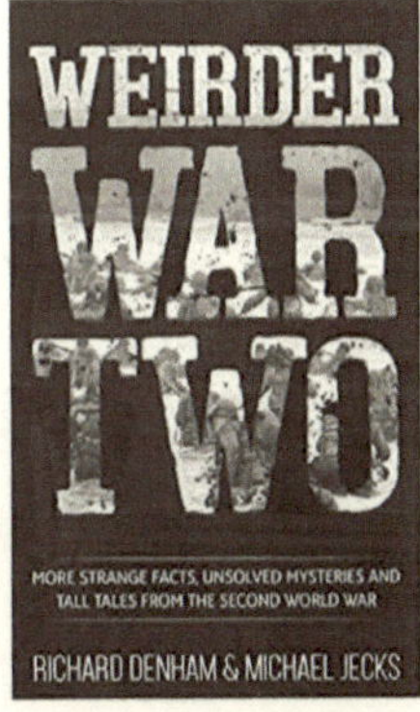

Weirder War Two by Richard Denham & Michael Jecks

'There are a terrible lot of lies going around the world, and the worst of it is half of them are true.'

- Winston Churchill

CONTENTS

FOREWORD

Weird; *out of the ordinary, strange, unusual…odd, bizarre, incomprehensible.*

New Shorter English Dictionary

First of all, a quick confession, this book isn't the 'weirdest' of the trilogy, the stories within are no more nor no less extraordinary than the first two books. However, I hope you will forgive this as 'weirdest' is a useful and appropriate title to end the series.

For those of you who have read 'Weird' and 'Weirder', it would be fair to be concerned that we have scraped the barrel of remarkable and unbelievable facts and tales from the Second World War, but to our surprise as much as anyone's, this simply isn't the case. For instance, there is a huge amount of facts written throughout the trilogy but never made the cut for a variety of reasons, be they to contentious, uncertain, upsetting or simply to ridiculous. There are also a dwindling few who live to this day, and mentioning their stories, of which we are only bystanders, felt wrong.

As with the first two books, it would be inappropriate to categorise this title as 'humour'. Some of the stories within are heartwarming, full of kindness, love, courage and dogged determination. Other stories are dark, distressing and contentious. But that is what history is. We live in a world where any question can be Googled and answered (up to a point) in seconds and the uncertainty of history doesn't always have a black and white answer. So much of history is opinion; 'history is written by the victors' rings truer than we know.

For example, depending on who you ask, the Soviet Union won the Second World single-handedly by withstanding the onslaught of Operation Barbarossa, courageously fighting to the end while the Western Allies sat and watched; or the war was only possible because Hitler secretly allied with Stalin in the Molotov-Ribbentrop pact, carving up eastern Europe between them (as seen in Poland) and freeing Hitler to turn his eye to the West, it was Soviet oil and Soviet grain that fed the German war machine. In a cruel twist of history, it is likely that Operation Barbarossa, and perhaps even Germany's ability to wage war, was only possible because of Soviet trade in the first place. A cold view is that undeniably the Soviet Union spent a third of the war on Nazi Germany's side, and spent two-thirds facing the brunt of Hitler's aggression.

Look at figures such as Winston Churchill, idolized by some, despised and condemned by others. At the very least he is a 'problematic' figure, but who isn't? No one comes out of history well; the ideas of the age never stay. Is it particularly fair to call him a racist imperialist when that's what most people thought at the time? We, in our age, will not escape this retrospective justice from generations to come. And like those before us, we will have no clue why. Perhaps future generations will be disgusted by our treatment of the planet, or the fact we eat the flesh of living creatures, and not being brave enough to do it ourselves, pay for workers in giant factories to slaughter animals for us. Perhaps we will be ridiculed for being so easily offended and upset, or chastised for not being offended and upset enough?

There is a very disturbing trend in recent years for censorship and a form of modern idolatry. Generations from now, I hope that they will look back at our time and find us bizarre and unreasonable for being offended by the past and trying to censor it. Who benefits from censoring films, adding 'trigger warnings' to old classics, tearing down statues of men and women long dead? Being involved in the murky world of history makes things even worse for us. For a broad example, the treatment of Africans during the Atlantic slave trade is no doubt horrific and should strike a chord with all of us, but how far do we spread our net? The treatment of African slaves in the Arab world was much larger and much more brutal, but the modern mob either doesn't know or doesn't understand that. Do we go even further, we live in a world where one wrong word or out-of-context tweet condemns a person to be 'cancelled', so it would be a brave one who raised the issue that Africa was the biggest market for African slaves, and they were enslaved by other Africans and then sold to other nations. The slave trade couldn't have happened without inter-tribal warfare. With all this talk of reparations, an obscene and inhuman idea that those alive now should take the blame for things their ancestors may have possibly been involved in the slave trade and compensate those alive who were never part of it. This is all uncomfortable reading, but it has to be. The cherry picking and selective outrage of history is one of the biggest dangers facing us.

And with all that said, we can begin to understand, whether we like it or not, that history, and the interpretation of it, can only be our own opinions. There is no search engine on Earth that can tell us what is and isn't morally justifiable and what is and isn't going to stand the test of time. Most of us will agree that the Second World War raged on between 1939-1945 (it's a different story in Asia etc.), but what happened, and why, within those six unbelievable years is a different story.

As always, I hope those of you with a strong interest in World War Two will forgive the whistle-stop tour nature of the book, and I hope those of you with a casual interest will forgive getting bogged down in dates and technical terms and perhaps not always providing enough context which would disturb the readers' flow. What we could like is for you to use this book as a starting block, and run off with those facts which interest or intrigue you, and make up your own mind from there – because that's all history ever can be.

A huge thank you to the talented M. J. Trow for collaborating with me on this project. His wealth of knowledge is admirable and his decades of expertise as a history teacher shine through to this day. The Weird War trilogy has been a part of both of our lives for over five years and a huge amount of painstaking research has been undertaken to make this series. Another huge thank you goes to Carol Trow, our long suffering conduit, editor and oracle who, with patience, humour and endurance, has not only mediated between two occasionally contrasting views, but also taken on the task of typing it up and generally keeping the peace!

Below each title, you will find one to three exclamations to demonstrate how weird we personally believe something was, from weird, to weirder, to weirdest.

Welcome, one last time, to Weird War Two…

Richard Denham

INTRODUCTION

The Second World War 1939-45

The Causes

The older generation still call it 'Hitler's War' but monumental events that lead to the deaths of millions cannot be placed at any one man's door. To understand how war came about in September 1939 we have to go back to the Treaty of Versailles that ended the First World War.

The victors at Versailles – Britain, France, Italy and the United States – decided that Germany had caused the First World War (which they hadn't) and that Germany must pay. To that end, territory which once belonged to Germany was taken away, German armed forces were cut to almost non-existence and the country was saddled with a massive reparations bill of £3.5 billion (at least $46 billion today) and it couldn't possibly pay.

The weak democratic Weimar government struggled on for ten years, but the financial disaster of October 1929 – the Wall Street crash – plunged Germany particularly deeply into recession and that gave a new impetus to Adolf Hitler's National Socialist party, which, until then, had been regarded as something of a lunatic fringe. In a series of underhand political manoeuvres, Hitler became Chancellor of Germany in 1933 and set up a state he promised would last a thousand years – the Third Reich. In fact, it lasted just twelve and a half years and the steps that led to the Second World War also led to Germany's second defeat in thirty years.

The Steps to War 1933-39

1933   Hitler becomes Chancellor of a bitter and angry Germany.

1934   On the death of President Hindenberg, Hitler becomes President, giving himself the title *Fuhrer* (leader).

All members of the German army (Wehrmacht), air force (Luftwaffe) and navy (Kriegsmarine) swear a personal oath of allegiance to Hitler.

1935   In an Anglo-German naval agreement, Germany is allowed to build warships again.

Saarland (Germany's smallest federal state) is returned to Germany after a referendum, having been removed from its control as part of the Treaty of Versailles.

1936   Hitler invades the demilitarized Rhineland, devoid of troops since Versailles, claiming that he has that right. Britain and France complain but do nothing.

Civil war breaks out in Spain and Hitler supplies General Francisco Franco's Fascists with aircraft, experts and cash. The Luftwaffe's Condor Legion bombs Guernica, giving the world the first taste of Blitzkrieg (Lightning War).

The Rome-Berlin Axis (the Pact of Steel) is signed between Hitler and Benito Mussolini, the Fascist duce (leader) of Italy, but not ratified until three years later.

Germany and Japan sign the Anti-Comintern Pact against the left wing countries of the Communist International, spearheaded by Russia (the Union of Socialist Soviet Republics).

1938   The *Anschluss* with Austria. On the face of it, a peaceful union, it is actually a Nazi coup.

Hitler claims the Sudetenland, part of the new state of Czechoslovakia, as German because of the large number of Germans living there. He needs *lebensraum* (living space) for his rapidly growing country.

At the Munich Conference in September, Hitler promises Neville Chamberlain, the British Prime Minister and Edouard Daladier, his French counterpart, that he has no further ambitions in Europe.

1939 Ignoring Munich, Hitler invades Prague and Memel in March.

Anxious to expand to the east and to regain East Prussia, Hitler signs a non-aggression pact with Josef Stalin, the Russian leader.

Two days later, Britain signs an agreement with Poland that is clearly Hitler's short-term target. On a pretext, on 1 September, Hitler launches *Fall Weiss* (Case White) and invades Poland.

On 3 September, with Hitler ignoring Chamberlain's ultimatum to withdraw his troops, Britain declares war on Nazi Germany. So does France.

The Second World War has begun.

The Phoney War 1939-40

The French called it the Funny War (Drôle de Guerre); to the Germans it was Sitzkrieg (the Armchair War). The British coined the word 'phoney' from an article by an American journalist based in London. In the west, nothing happened. The east was a different story, however. Poland fell in the September War, crushed between Hitler's Germany and Stalin's Russia and the execution squads of the einsatzgruppen went to work rounding up and shooting Jews – another step towards the Holocaust.

There was action at sea too. Two British aircraft carriers, the newest and most expensive ships afloat, had been sunk by October, and there were air raids on British naval bases in Scotland. The Kriegsmarine's pocket battleship, the *Admiral Graf Spee* was scuttled by her crew in the River Plate on 17 December. In terms of military capability, the Royal Navy had the edge, but the Luftwaffe, whose aircraft had been built secretly for years, were far ahead of the Royal Air Force, thanks to years of appeasement under Prime Ministers Baldwin and Chamberlain. In November, the USSR invaded Finland. This was the Winter War, in which the Finns, with their local knowledge, proved more than a match for the Red Army.

With spectacular mistiming, Neville Chamberlain told that House of Commons that, in delaying an all-out attack in the west, Hitler had 'missed the bus'. Five days later, the Germans invaded Norway.

Collapse of the West 1940

It was the British who had misread the bus timetable! Norway was crucial to both sides, because of its strategic position overlooking the North Atlantic and its production of heavy water. The Germans moved first and despite a half-hearted British involvement, overran the country and set up a puppet government under Vidkun Quisling, whose name became synonymous with traitor (in fact, he had never made any secret of his Nazi sympathies). Denmark, hopelessly feeble against the power of the Reich, surrendered after only one day and the threat to flatten Copenhagen. Of the 16,000 troops in the Danish army, only thirteen were killed.

Failure in Norway led to a no-confidence vote in the Commons and Chamberlain was forced to resign. His replacement, on 10 May, was the First Lord of the Admiralty, Winston Churchill. He had been warning of the Nazi threat for years and this was to be his finest hour.

Churchill's first day at Number Ten was the start of *Fall Gelb* (Case Yellow), the simultaneous invasion of Holland, Belgium and France. On paper, the Allied and Axis armies were exactly matched but no one was prepared for the speed of the German advance under blitzkrieg. Aerial attacks, using a mixture of bombers (*Heinkels* and *Dorniers*) and fighters (*Messerschmitts* and *Stukas*) were followed by pincer movements on the ground spearheaded by the *panzers*, the tanks that had replaced horsed cavalry. The Allies had no leaders of the calibre of Heinz Guderian, Erwin Rommel and Gerd von

Rundstedt and despite valiant defence, Holland surrendered in five days.

A British expeditionary force was rushed to France (exactly as in 1914) but was driven back to the coast at Dunkirk. The 'miracle' that happened there was the result of private boats – 'the little ships of England' – that crossed the Channel and carried back as many men as they could. It was all part of Churchill's genius that he turned what was actually an embarrassing defeat into a victory and the 'Dunkirk spirit' is still occasionally heard of today. Belgium surrendered at the end of May and France soon after. The armistice was signed in the same railway carriage at Compiegne where the Germans had surrendered in 1918 and an ecstatic Hitler went sightseeing in Paris. Versailles was avenged.

The People's War 1940-41

The summer of 1940 has become the 'Spitfire Summer'. Hitler's invasion of Britain – Operation Sealion – was heralded by the blitzkrieg tactic of knocking out the RAF first. All over the south east of the country, dogfights were fought daily in what became known as the Battle of Britain, but the RAF – 'the few' as Churchill called them – held out and Herman Goering, head of the Luftwaffe, was forced to change tack and bomb civilian cities instead.

'The Blitz', beginning in earnest on 30 August, is a prime example of Britain's 'finest hour'. Guernica came to London, Coventry, Plymouth and Hull. Industrial, war production areas were the target but the bombing technology of 1940 was not that precise and homes, schools, hospitals and *people* were all caught up in it. A paranoid government, convinced that there was a Fifth Column of spies operating in the country, gave draconian powers to the police, the armed forces and an army of 'little Hitlers' in and out of uniform, to curb civil liberties. Much of this has never gone away. Bombing raids, the blackout, spivs selling rationed goods illegally on the black market, all this became part of a legend. By May 1941, 40,000 British civilians had been killed, another 46,000 badly injured. Over a million homes were shattered. But the world learned a lesson that still has to be driven home – mass bombing does not lead to collapse; it just increases resistance.

The Wider War 1941-42
Countries overrun by the Germans coped as best they could. Most people kept their heads down and did as they were told. Some collaborated openly – Quisling in Norway, Marshal Petain in Vichy France. Others resisted, either passively or actively, like the Maquis in France, sabotaging German occupation and staying in touch by radio with Britain, now 'fortress Britain', standing alone.

With dreams of recreating another Roman Empire, Mussolini sent his troops into North Africa in June 1940. Egypt had been in British hands since the nineteenth century and General Archibald Wavell stopped the Italians at Sidi Birrani in December. It was depressing proof to Hitler that his Italian allies weren't worth the candle and he sent in Erwin Rommel and his Afrika Korps to bail them out. Wavell was beaten back.

The extraordinarily tortuous politics of the Balkans re-emerged, resulting in a German attack on the new state of Yugoslavia (today's Croatia) and the invasion of Greece. The British attempt to police the Mediterranean (they had Gibraltar at the western end, Malta in the centre and Cyprus in the east) met with disaster and Crete fell to the Germans by June 1941.

On the 22nd of that month, Hitler made the biggest mistake of the war by launching Operation Barbarossa, the invasion of the USSR. This had been his plan all along, taking *lebensraum* to a logical conclusion and Josef Stalin seemed blissfully unaware. The long drawn out Eastern Front saw the deaths of millions. To the Russians, it was the Patriotic War, defending their own territory against a treacherous enemy. Stalin was quite prepared to sacrifice as many millions as it took. For their part, the Germans had underestimated both the tenacity of the enemy and the severity of the Russian winter. Petrol froze in the tanks of mechanised transport and blitzkrieg ground to a halt in sieges like Stalingrad.

On 7 December – 'a day that will live in infamy' as President Franklin D Roosevelt said – the Japanese bombed the US naval base at Pearl Harbor in the Hawaiian Islands. America had sat on an isolationist fence throughout the Twenties and Thirties, its population made up of the descendants of both sides who faced each other in 1939. Roosevelt's natural inclination was to join the Allies but there was a powerful German lobby at home and he had promised America's mothers that their boys would not be involved. Instead, the Lend-Lease programme was set up – vital money and equipment lent to Britain (the debt was finally repaid in 1994).

Japanese ambitions in the Pacific (they had been at war with China since 1937) were unrealistic. America's actual military strength in 1941 was feeble, but the wealth of the country and its military capability were awesome. The 'double whammy' of Barbarossa and Pearl Harbor in the same year made it inevitable that Hitler would lose the war.

Initially, the Japanese did well, driving the British out of Singapore in one of the most embarrassing defeats in modern history. The creation of the Burma railway, where thousands of British prisoners of war were worked to death, ranks alongside the Holocaust in terms of inhumanity, although of course the numbers going routinely to the gas chambers of Europe by 1943 have no comparison.

Now that Soviet Russia had joined the Allied camp, there was need to relieve them as far as possible. Convoys of British merchant ships ploughed the icy waters of the North Atlantic to achieve this, at the mercy of the dreaded Kriegsmarine U Boats. A huge propaganda coup was struck when the iconic new battleship the *Bismarck* was sunk by the British in May 1941.

Turning Points 1942-43

We have already seen how important Hitler's decision to invade Russia was. The attack on Pearl Harbor was another gamble too far. In the Pacific, the Americans fought back at the battle of Midway, in which the Japanese lost four aircraft carriers, 332 aircraft and 3,500 men.

In July, Bernard Montgomery's British Eighth Army stopped Rommel's Afrika Korps at El Alamein, near Alexandria and Operation Torch saw the invasion of Italian-held Morocco, Algeria and Tunisia by the British and Americans.

In the east, the Wehrmacht was losing men daily at an horrific rate and by 31 January 1943, General Friedrich von Paulus was forced to surrender the Sixth Army.

The Invasion of Europe 1942-44

With Rommel's Afrika Korps destroyed and the Italians on the run, an Anglo-American force invaded Sicily and Italy, making for Rome. It was the first assault of Hitler's Europe-wide Reich and one of its first casualties was Mussolini, kicked out by his own government and put under house arrest. Stiffened by the Germans, Italy held on for months, fighting battles at Anzio and Monte Cassino, but in the end, they surrendered and were effectively out of the war by the end of 1943.

In the summer of that year, the Red Army under General Georgy Zhukov began to push the exhausted Wehrmacht back to the German border they had crossed with such high hopes during Barbarossa two years earlier. Zhukov's ultimate destination was Berlin.

For the RAF it was payback time. With the USAAF flying out from British bases, Air Chief Marshal Arthur 'Bomber' Harris unleashed raids on German cities. Dresden was hit by a firestorm unparalleled in history and today Harris is regarded by many as a war criminal. In fact, he was just doing his job and no one at the time had a problem with that.

All of this was crowned on 6 June 1944 by Operation Overlord, the biggest amphibious assault in history. 27,000 airborne troops had landed in Normandy the previous night to take vital bridgeheads and road crossings before the 'ducks' ran up the beaches codenamed Omaha, Utah, Sword, Gold and Juno. The Germans were caught napping. Only at 'bloody Omaha' was there serious resistance; Rommel was on leave in Germany at the time and Hitler dithered. The next weeks after D Day (D for Deliverance) saw the Allies driving the Wehrmacht across France, liberating towns and villages as they went.

The Race for Berlin 1944-45

By the end of September 1944, twenty-five of thirty-seven German divisions of Army Group Centre had been destroyed by the Red Army. Berlin was panicking – the Cossacks were on the German border and the Communist threat had never loomed so starkly. By the end of the year, the Germans had pulled out of the Balkans, consolidating and regrouping to defend their homeland.

1944 saw a sting in the tail with the return of the Blitz over Britain. Hitler's rocket scientists, working on jet and unmanned aircraft technology, came out with the V1 and V2 missiles – 'doodlebugs' – that rained down on British cities as conventional bombs had three years earlier.

Advancing steadily from the west, the Allies, under the command of General Dwight Eisenhower, drove all before them. There were disagreements as to how exactly this should be done and hotheads like Montgomery and George Patton constantly clashed. Operation Market Garden, an airborne attempt to capture the bridges at Arnhem, was a disaster however with a loss of life that was all the harder to take because the end of the war was now surely in sight. In a last ditch gamble, the Germans attacked in the Ardennes forest – the battle of the Bulge. Probably only a lack of equipment meant that it failed.

At the beginning of 1945, Hitler became increasingly delusional. The Allies crossed the Rhine in February and March as the Russians swept through eastern Germany to take territory they would refuse to give up for forty years. In the event, it was the Red Army that got to Berlin first, fighting street by street for the enemy capital. The names of some of them are still there, scratched into the plaster of the

Reichstag, Berlin's parliament building. In an appalling act which the Russians still deny, thousands of German women and girls were raped by Soviet troops.

Gotterdammerung 1945

Hitler was hiding in his bunker under Berlin while the fighting raged overhead. On 29 April he married his mistress Eva Braun and they committed suicide, either by poison or gunshot (exact details are unclear) and their bodies were doused in petrol and burned. Admiral Karl Doenitz was Hitler's successor, all other leading Nazis now on the run and he negotiated the Reich's surrender over the next few days. 8 May was officially designated VE (Victory in Europe) Day and there were street parties all over Britain and the newly-liberated countries of the west.

In the far east, General William Slim's 14th Army drove the Japanese out of Burma and the Americans captured island after island in the South Pacific ('island hopping', it was called). Iwo Jima and Okinawa became enshrined in American folklore as a result but it was felt that everyone was too exhausted to go on; and to the Japanese, surrender was unthinkable. With that in mind, the new president, Harry S Truman, authorised the first use of the newly-created atomic bomb. 'Little Boy' and 'Fat Man' flattened the cities of Hiroshima and Nagasaki, bringing nuclear terror to the world with which we all still live. In seventeen seconds at Hiroshima, 80,000 people were dead with a further 70,000 badly injured. VJ Day (Victory in Japan) was officially 15 August.

What next?

As the Allies liberated German-held Europe, the reality of the Holocaust came to light. Six million people, Jews, homosexuals, gypsies and political dissidents had been exterminated in death camps like Auschwitz, Dachau and Treblinka. The Nazi high command scattered but most of them were captured and faced trial for war crimes at Nuremberg, the scene of the pre-war Nazi rallies, in 1946.

Sixteen of the twenty-one were hanged by the British executioner Albert Pierrepoint.

Various high level Allied conferences over the last two years of the war set out the post-war world. Soviet Russia refused to hand back captured German territories and used the war as an opportunity to extend the limits of the Soviet bloc to include large sections of eastern Europe that had never been either Communist or Russian. Germany itself was divided between the Allies, east and west Berlin suffering the same fate. Winston Churchill, ousted in a post-war election, prophesied that an 'iron curtain' would come down across Europe and so it proved, leading to the Cold War and espionage fictions without number.

A devastated world struggled to come to terms with what had happened, rebuilding, reshaping and trying to forget the past. But some things – the Holocaust, the blanket bombing, the Burma railway, the A bomb – are unforgettable. We will always have them with us.

THE BATTLE OF THE TENNIS COURT

!

Think of Thermopylae and you think of Leonidas and his three hundred Spartans facing impossible odds against the Persians in narrow mountain passes. Think of Stalingrad and you have a ghastly image of death and destruction when the might of the Wehrmacht broke against the immovable wall of the Red Army.

But there is another battle, unknown alongside Thermopylae and Stalingrad, a battle voted by the National Army Museum in London in 2013 as the greatest battle ever fought by the British. It is the battle of Kohima, the battle of the tennis court.

The war in Burma, today's Myanmar, was brutal, if only because the Japanese had a different mindset to the West. The little country had punched above its weight taking on China in the 1930s and the attack on Pearl Harbor brought the opposition of the United States. On 4 April 1944, as part of their push towards British India, the 31st Japanese Division encircled the British position at Kohima. With the town cut off, the Commonwealth forces were running low on water and three days later the 161st Brigade of General Montague Stopford's XXXIII Corps were later surrounded at Jotsoma near the town.

The District Commissioner's bungalow came under attack on 8 April and drove the British back to the nearest high ground, the tennis court. This was hand-to-hand combat at its most lethal, one British Tommy buried temporarily under the mud and the bodies of his comrades. He played dead until dark, then dug his way out and dashed back across the tarmac to his own lines.

Attacks came every half an hour, including mortar fire directed at the field hospital in full view of the tennis courts themselves. Time was of the essence for two reasons. General William Slim of the 14th Army was bound to send help (it came first in the form of aerial support) and the monsoon season was about to break, after which all military operations would be severely compromised.

From their entrenched positions on either side of the tennis court, the Allies and the Japanese hurled grenades at each other, like a bizarre centre court at Wimbledon. Air drops were not that effective, ammunition and water landing in thick jungle and often ending up in the hands of the Japanese. When Stopford's tanks arrived, the onslaught continued until 10 May when the Japanese were driven back.

The war cemetery in Kohima has 1,420 graves to Allied soldiers. It was built on the site of that tennis court in the Commissioner's bungalow's garden and carved into the central memorial there are the now famous and poignant lines –

'When you go home, tell them of us and say,
For your tomorrow, we gave our today.'

THE BEE BOMBS OF PRESTER JOHN

!!

Prester John (John the Priest) never existed. He was believed throughout the Middle Ages and much later, to be a Christian king who lived in the far east and would one day (he was immortal) save the crusading west against Islam. By the nineteenth century the legend still stood, but he was now an ancestor of the Selassie rulers of Ethiopia in East Africa. The Rastafarian cult of which the emperor Haile Selassie was the leader, believed the man to be a messiah and were as appalled as their emperor when European politics muscled its way into their territory.

Benito Mussolini, Italy's Fascist dictator, wanted to create a new Roman Empire and one obvious place to do it was in a backward society like Ethiopia. War broke out over this in October 1935 and a horrified world's press carried reports of natives armed with spears and shields, trying to hold back a modern, mechanical Italian army bent on destruction.

Haile Selassie himself, dignified and solemn, with complete justification on his side, appeared before the League of Nations to demand justice. The League had been set up after the First World War to arbitrate such international disputes, but it had no teeth and proved itself wholly inadequate. Adolf Hitler, for instance (now teaching Mussolini a lesson by sending guns to the Ethiopians) refused to join the League and simply ignored them.

Having to cope as best they could, the Ethiopians came up with an ancient weapon of which Prester John (had he ever lived!) would have approved. Soldiers would jump on to Italian tanks and throw a bee-hive into the vehicle's sights before getting out, fast. Pandemonium ensued when terrified Italians could be seen baling out of their tanks, much to the delight of Haile Selassie's men.

THE BIELSKI BROTHERS

!

The casualty rate in the countries caught between Nazi Germany and Soviet Russia was horrific. In Belorussia, tens of thousands of Jews were murdered and the rest forced into ghettos which were duly 'liquidated' in 1942-3.

Such would have been the fate of the entire Bielski family who were hanged or machine-gunned in the Nowogrodek ghetto in December 1941; except that four of the family's six sons – Tuvia, Asael, Zus and Aharon – escaped and took about thirty others with them. Knowing the local geography like the backs of their hands, the boys disappeared in the impenetrable forests of Zabiedovo and Peralaz. They linked up with Soviet partisans and stole weapons. Tuvia became the leader of a warband that had twentieth century parallels with Robin Hood, striking a blow for freedom against the evil sheriff of Nottingham in Sherwood Forest. He sent agents into the ghettos, recruiting people and escorting them back to the hideout. That way, 100 Jews who would otherwise have died at Iwie were saved. By the summer of 1943, the 'merry men' had grown to an astonishing 700 people! Naturally, this irked the Germans. Twenty thousand Einsatzgruppen and Wehrmacht troops were unleashed, hunting for the Bielskis. There was a price of 100,000 Reichsmarks on Tuvia's head. From their base in the Nalikoki Forest, the group set up their own mill, laundry, school, synagogue and courthouse. They joined partisan Resistance groups, attacked collaborators and targeted the police, using explosives to sabotage bridges and railways.

By the time Stalin's Red Army had driven the Germans out of Belorussia in the summer of 1944, the Bielski group was 1,230 strong, 70 per cent of them women, children and the elderly. They travelled back to Nowogrodek and disbanded.

Like many Belorussians, at the end of the war they realised that in welcoming the Red Army, the Bielskis had simply swapped one vicious dictatorship for another. Asael was killed, fighting as a Soviet conscript in February 1945. The others fled west, fighting for the new state of Israel in 1948 and then to New York. The last survivor, Aharon, still lives in Florida.

The extraordinary life of Belorussia's Robin Hood was told in the 2009 film *Defiance*, starring Daniel Craig as Tuvia.

THE BLACK BEAST

!!

Pal was a Newfoundland, one of the huge dogs bred for haulage across the frozen wastes of northern Canada. He belonged to the Hayden family, and although gentle, like all his breed, he had scratched the face of the family's 6-year-old, so he had to go. It was a tough decision. Should he be put down or merely moved on? In the end, sentimentality prevailed, and Pal was taken to the Royal Canadian Air Force station at Gander. Accordingly, that became his new name and he was officially instated as the regimental mascot of the 1st Battalion, Royal Canadian Rifles. A dog as loyal and intelligent as Gander was bound to impress; within weeks, he was promoted to sergeant!

At the end of 1941, the Rifles found themselves fighting in unfamiliar territory, defending the British base of Hong Kong against a determined Japanese attack. This was not the Allies' finest hour. The defenders outnumbered the Japanese and should have been able to hold on, but aerial support was lacking and the British surrendered on Christmas Day.

Rifleman Fred Kelly may well have been a formidable fighter, but he took his helmet off to his dog, Sergeant Gander, who was up to his neck in the hand to paw fighting at street level. Three times he drove the Japanese back, snapping at their heels as they ran. When the attackers interrogated prisoners later, they wanted to know about the 'black beast' that had run amok through their ranks, fearing that the Canadians were training such animals as killers.

Gander's number came up in the fight at Lei Yue

Mun, the narrow channel leading to Hong Kong's harbour. A group of Canadians, trying to hold off a renewed assault, were under heavy fire, with a number of casualties. When a hand grenade hurtled through the air, the dog grabbed the pineapple in his powerful jaws and dashed towards the enemy lines. He was fast, but not fast enough and the grenade exploded, killing him instantly. His human handlers, however, lived to fight another day.

One thousand nine hundred and seventy-seven Canadians died at Hong Kong and Gander's name is listed with them. His medal is on display in Ottawa's Canadian War Museum and there is a statue to him and Rifleman Kelly at Gander Heritage Memorial Park, unveiled in July 2015. The fighting man's best friend was awarded the Dicken Medal for Gallantry by the People's Dispensary for Sick Animals in October 2000. Twenty veterans of the Rifles were there that day.

THE BLACK BOOK

!!

One of the sharpest brains in the German secret service (Sicherheitsdienst or SD) was Walter Schellenberg who became, during the later stages of the war, Hitler's spymaster. In 1940 he was deputy leader of Amt IV of the Reich Central Security Office in Berlin, responsible for counter-intelligence. Not only had he captured two top British agents in the Venlo incident on the Dutch border, he was also the mastermind behind Operation Willi, an attempt to coerce the exiled Duke of Windsor (Edward VIII) into the Nazi cause.

Schellenberg's task in the spring of 1941 was to compile the Sonderfahndingsliste-GB (Special search list, Great Britain), effectively a death-list for known opponents of the Reich in the UK, later known as Hitler's Book or the Black Book. It was typed up, complete with entries by secretaries at SD headquarters, in Wilhemstrasse, Berlin while Spitfires and Messerschmitts were slogging it out over the skies of Southern England.

A similar list, containing 61,000 names, had already been compiled for Poland and most of those on it who had not been able to escape the onslaught of the Wehrmacht and the einsatzgruppen, were dead. For those who today question whether the British version was actually a death list, this fact alone speaks volumes.

The 2,694 people in the Black Book could be divided into a number of categories. Inevitably, Britain's political leaders were there, men like Churchill, the Prime Minister and his deputy, Clement Attlee. Neville Chamberlain is there too, even though he was now seriously ill, semi-retired from politics and had, after all, appeased Hitler for most of the past seven years. Ernest Bevin, the Minister of Labour was B131. Alfred Duff Cooper, the Minister of Information, was D114. And there were the 'B' feature men, like Harold MacMillan, the future prime minister; Edwin Duncan-Sandys, the future Foreign Secretary. Women, who held virtually no place in the Nazi hierarchy, are not forgotten. Sylvia Pankhurst is listed, as a feminist and former suffragette, as is Megan Lloyd-George, the daughter of the prime minister of the First World War who was rather impressed with Hitler in the '30s. There was a galaxy of consuls, vice-consuls, envoys and attaches, 'our men' in various countries who had annoyed Hitler's regime in any number of ways. The leader of the eight exiled governments hiding in London (hardly the safest place in the world by September 1940) are on the list, along with their hangers-on. Charles De Gaulle of the Free French; Edouard Benes of the Czech Republic; Wladyslaw Sikorski of the Polish army.

There is of course, a large group in the Black Book who are emigres, intellectuals and politicians who got out of Europe while they still could. Many of these were Jews and British minorities were singled out for destruction come the German invasion because they had given them jobs. And there were home-grown British dissidents too – the left wing publisher Victor Gollancz; Harold Laski; the Socialist liberal, Bertrand Russell, already the grand old man of philosophy.

Institutions, as well as individuals came under Schellenberg's scrutiny. The public schools, as well as the universities, bred the officer class currently leading the war effort against the Reich. Boy Scouts and Girl Guides help with that war effort too. Most businessmen were in league (shock! Horror!) with Churchill and Beaverbrook's shackling of the economy to win the war. Those were traitors in Britain, good Germans who should know better. Spies, naturally, could not be allowed to survive.

Today we tend to scoff at the Nazis with hugely

popular TV sitcoms like *Dad's Army* and *'Allo! 'Allo!* and we focus on the mistakes in the Black Book. Albert Einstein, probably the greatest genius of his generation, had fled Germany, but merely bounced in and out of Britain before going to America; Schellenberg believed he was still there. Churchill is listed twice; so is Attlee. And Freud, the famous psychoanalyst, was already dead.

The other side of the coin, however, is terrifying. Given the limited access to information across the Channel because of the war, the Nazis were extraordinarily well-informed. They had aliases, circles of friends and acquaintances, telephone numbers, addresses, even car registration numbers, all of which would have been used to hunt dissidents down in the event of a German invasion.

Let us leave the last word, however, to one of the several 'luvvies' on the list. After the war, when one of the two copies (of 20,000 published) was discovered and the story hit the British press, the novelist Rebecca West sent a telegram to fellow listee, Noel Coward – 'My dear,' she wrote, 'the people we should have been seen dead with.'

THE BOSTON HERALD RUMOR CLINIC

!!!

Imagine the horror as an American mother opened a parcel addressed to her, only to find her captured son's eyes staring up at her. Imagine the terror of the people of Curry County, Oregon when they heard that a bomb had exploded in their area, releasing deadly plague bacteria. It was widely known that 90% of the women who served in the Women's Auxiliary Army Corps were prostitutes. Native American soldiers, at Fort Devon, armed and no doubt under the influence of 'fire water', had gone on the rampage, raping any white woman in sight. A woman who had spent a small fortune to have her hair permed, walked into her day job in a munitions factory and her head exploded. And, of course, not a single American ship escaped the Japanese aerial attack on Pearl Harbor.

Nothing in the paragraph above is true. They are all fine examples of 'fake news' long before the phrase came into being. Misinformation and disinformation have been the bane of governments' existence for centuries. When the stones of St. Paul's Cathedral in London exploded because of the heat of the great fire in 1666, people swore they saw French warships bombarding the building from the river Thames. Attempts to damp down on this sort of nonsense have usually met with failure.

One man who tried was journalist Frances Sweeney who wrote regularly for *Life* magazine and *Readers' Digest*. She created the Boston Herald Rumor Clinic, using around 300 'morale workers' to keep their eyes open and their ears to the ground to hunt down tall tales. But there was an irony here. If, just for a moment, you were tempted to believe anything you read in the opening paragraph, that is because it is human nature to do so. The mere reporting of such stories, even when they are debunked, give them oxygen and the United States Office of War Information criticised Sweeney for that reason.

The criticism which could be levelled at the government is that so little information was being released. It was not until ten weeks after Pearl Harbor that President Roosevelt gave out details in one of his famous 'fireside chats' over the radio.

And sometimes, of course, governments lied to their people for the sake of morale. On 10 May 1941, the heaviest blitz of the war rained down on London. The BBC the next day, told a terrified nation (who rarely missed a broadcast) that 28 enemy aircraft had been shot down. In fact, the real total was a measly seven. But somehow, 28 sounded a better balance against the destruction on the ground.

Nazis dressed in nuns' habits patrolled the English countryside. Collaborators were lighting the way for the Luftwaffe with cigarette lighters. The Germans were digging a tunnel under the Channel to surprise the people of Kent. Women were attacking parachutists with pitchforks, stealing their silk to make nylons and knickers. You'd better believe it!!

CARROT ON A STICK

!

The Second World War hit ordinary people like no other in history. Because of the range of enemy bombers, everybody's home was the Front Line. And even without the Blitz, privation became the order of the day. The Ministry of Food was set up to control the production and intake of food. Rationing, coupons, queues – they became the 'new normal' from 1940 until, in some cases, long after the war was over.

The 'Dig for Victory' campaign encouraged people to turn their lawns and flower gardens into allotments; even the greens of the Tower of London where umpteen Tudors had lost their heads, were planted with vegetables. Pig clubs were set up, 6,000 animals sharing gardens throughout the land; even the Metropolitan Police had one. The family pet was no longer a cat or a tortoise, but a chicken or a rabbit because they were edible. Vegetables, fruit, fish and above all, bread were never rationed, because of the panic that that might cause. But everything was in chronically short supply; by the end of 1942, Britain had lost 728,000 tonnes of imported food to U-boat attacks.

Enter good old British 'make do and mend'. No lemonade? Never mind, just grate carrots and swede, strain them through muslin and you have Carrotade. And don't forget curried carrot, carrot puddings and carrot jam. If you freeze the carrot juice, you can have carrot on a stick. Given the few domestic fridges in Britain during the war, this was luxury indeed.

And of course, the Ministry of |Information insisted, carrots helped you see at night – Bomber command never took off without them. The *real* all-seeing 'eye' – radar – was top secret, known only to a select few in the RAF and Air Ministry. In the States, Walt Disney was doing his bit for this propaganda – Carroty George, Clara Carrot and Pop Carrot all appeared in the cartoons of 1942 and in Britain, kids could rely on the ubiquitous 'Doctor Carrot', 'the children's best friend', ably assisted by his sidekick Potato Pete.

Carrots even found their way into the codes used by the Maquis and other French Resistance groups. As D-day loomed – and happened – on 6 June 1944, wireless sets all over France crackled 'les carottes sont cuites' (the carrots are cooked).

Long after the war, exasperated parents would still try to get food into their uninterested toddlers' mouths by making aircraft noises and calling out patriotically 'One for the king'.

CHEERS!

!!

Deception has been part of the art of war since the Chinese strategist Sun Tzu wrote his book of the same name in the fifth century BC. Shakespeare makes much of Macduff's army using trees as a defence, bringing to reality the omen that 'Birnham wood shall come to Dunsinane' to defeat the tyrant Macbeth. In the real (medieval) world, Edward, Prince of Wales raised false standards to make his enemy, Simon de Montfort, believe that friends were on their way to rescue him at Evesham in 1265. In the build up to D-Day, in June 1945, inflatable tanks were scattered in various parts of northern England to confuse spotter aircraft into believing that Operation Overlord would be delivered in Norway.

The Germans had their own deception plan. They built fake airfields, including runways, buildings and 'parked' planes. The idea was to lure Allied bombers to waste their bombs on unimportant fields. As far as their real airfields were concerned, they painted bomb damage on perfectly usable buildings to make bomber crews believe there was no point in hitting them again. We must understand that bomb accuracy in the Second World War was nothing like it is today and that most bombs were dropped in relatively cloudy weather from 30,000 feet.

You cannot, however, con a conman. The Allies became wise to all this and dropped wooden bombs onto the wooden airfields, just to make a point. One German airman, who saw the funny side of all this, wanted to buy a drink for

the pilot who had dropped fake bombs onto his fake airfield.
The question is, would it have been a real drink?

'CLUTTY'

!

We are all familiar with Q of the James Bond franchise, an earnest, white-coated boffin (played usually by Desmond Llewellyn) who has invented the most cunning and brilliant gadgets and is exasperated by Bond who appears that he could not care less. Inevitably, though, the world's most famous spy ends up using the relevant gadget to foil his enemies, stay alive and, of course, make the world a safer place.

Perhaps the closest we can come to a real life Q was Clayton 'Clutty' Hutton, a pilot in the First World War who became fascinated by magic and escapology. He once had a bet with the famous escapologist Harry Houdini that the magician could not escape from a particular trap. Hutton knew he was on to a winner because he had given Houdini's maintenance crew a back-hander to fix the bolts!

When the Second World War loomed, Hutton joined M19, the branch of the Secret Service most concerned with espionage gadgetry to do with escape and evasion. By 1942 he had written the manual, a top secret list of his inventions called *Per Ardua Ad Libertes* (Through Hardship to Freedom). It was rumoured that he set up his workshop under a cemetery so that he would not be disturbed!

In his autobiography *Official Secret*, published in the United States in 1961 because no British publisher would touch it for security reasons, Hutton spelt out the ingenious ideas that he came up with. Prisoners of war in Germany and elsewhere were allowed to receive parcels. These came in the

Red Cross, but others were accepted too, once they had been checked by the camp authorities. Under bogus aliases such as the Welsh Provident Fund, the Licensed Victuallers' Sports Association and the Jigsaw Puzzle Club, M19 sent valuable 'get out of Stalag' cards which took a variety of forms. Packs of playing cards had maps hidden in them. Pilots' navigation charts were stashed inside the heels of shoes. Compasses were secreted behind buttons. Perhaps the most ingenious of all was the hijacking of the popular board game, Monopoly. The government did a secret deal with Waddingtons, the game's manufacturers, which had brilliant secrets all over the board. A full stop after 'Marylebone Station' was destined for Italy with hidden escape routes over the Alps. A full stop after 'Mayfair' was the version sent to Norway so that escapees could get to neutral Sweden. Some boards had real gold tokens (top hats and so on) that could be used as barter by escapees; and most daring of all, some of the Monopoly money was actual German currency, the Deutschmarks of which Hitler was so proud.

Q would have been proud too!

THE COOLER

!

If you are of a certain age, you will remember the cult television series of the 1960s, *The Prisoner*, starring Patrick McGoohan. The central character, known only as Number Six ('I am not a number; I am a free man!') is imprisoned in a surreal 'village' (Portmeirion in North Wales) and subjected to endless interrogation about what he knows. He is an agent who has fallen foul of his masters and knows too much top-secret 'stuff' to be allowed his freedom.

The writer of *The Prisoner* was George Markstein, a German Jew who fled to Britain as Hitler's grip on his native country became intolerable. And his own experiences meant that Number Six's predicament – the spy who knew too much – was not far removed from reality.

Espionage was a very impressive science. Many agents were incompetent or events overtook them, which led to their being compromised and of no further use to their handlers/spymasters. The Special Operations Executive (SOE) faced this problem by requisitioning Inverlair Lodge, a stately home in Scotland known officially as Number Six Special Workshop School and unofficially as 'the cooler', American criminal slang for solitary confinement.

Here, ex-agents were given comfortable accommodation (like McGoohan's prisoner) and, to make them feel useful, they worked behind the scenes on fictional missions which would keep them busy until the war ended. It could only ever be a temporary solution. Every Intelligence officer had signed the Official Secrets Act which meant that they had to keep their mouths shut. After the war, however, with politics changing by the week, several of them forgot that and rushed into print with their explosive memoirs.

THE COLDITZ COCK

!!

The story of Colditz is the stuff of Boys' Own adventure. The prison for 'incorrigible' Allied officers in Saxony was the plotline for a hugely popular film *The Colditz Story* and a long-running BBC drama – *Colditz* – in the 1970s. Both were based on Pat Reid's memoirs, as an inmate himself, and the exploits caught the imagination of several generations.

The Geneva Convention insisted that prisoners of war be treated with dignity and even courtesy. It was all a far cry from the treatment doled out to civilians in concentration camps throughout Europe, but the Germans by and large honoured it. Putting determined escapees together in one place made some sense, so that not every camp was infected with them; but policing a place like Colditz was a nightmare.

There were at least 186 escape attempts, 32 of them resulting in a 'home run' in which the escapees got to a friendly or neutral destination. It was a British officer's duty to try to escape; and a German guard's duty to stop him. It was all in the methodology. Any prisoner using forged or stolen German papers and impersonating a German soldier risked a firing squad; otherwise, it was all rather gentlemanly. This changed in 1944 when a Fuhrer order specified that commandos captured behind enemy lines were to be shot on sight.

Because of its layout, the Renaissance castle at Colditz was thought to be impregnable, perched high in the Saxon mountains. But there is a difference between a castle that is difficult to attack and one that does not leak its prisoners! In the castle library was a book called *Aircraft Design* which gave an enterprising escapee like Lieutenant Goldfinch not only the idea, but a blueprint for a plane. If you cannot tunnel your way out through rock and masonry using not much more than a teaspoon, how about flying out? They built a false wall in the prison attic behind which the 'hangar' gave birth to a glider, the *Colditz Cock*. A small team of technical men, largely Royal Engineers, calling themselves the Apostles, built the thing, with a further forty taking shifts as lookouts for patrolling, nosy guards.

The aircraft's ribs were made from bed-slats. The wing spars had once been floorboards and control wires were electric cables. The 'skin' was made from cotton sheets and sleeping bags. When it was finished, the *Cock* was 19 feet from nose to tail and had a 32 foot wingspan. How the guards could have failed to find something that size and to be totally unaware of its existence is beyond belief.

The problem, of course, was how to launch the *Cock*. In the event, history intervened, either depriving the world of a flash of true genius (had it worked) or deep embarrassment (if it didn't!). The American army spoiled the fun by liberating the camp on 16 April 1945.

The fate of the *Cock* is unknown. Since Colditz effectively disappeared behind Stalin's Iron Curtain in 1946, it was never seen again. One photograph of it exists, however. It was taken by American war correspondent Lee Carson and one of the Apostles, the aptly named Mr Goldfinch, had retained his drawings. Accordingly, a ⅓ scale model based on these was flown from Colditz castle in 1993, by which time there were no guards to object!

THE CURSE OF THE
WILLIE DEE

!!!

Sailors are a notoriously suspicious lot. Stories of mermaids, St. Elmo's Fire, Leviathans and the edge of the world, have been swapped in portside taverns for centuries. Old tars today are still not very happy about women serving on Royal Navy ships in the British Service.

In the Second World War a focus of this superstition was the *USS William D. Porter*, a Fletcher-class destroyer known with much affection, as '*Willie Dee*'. In November 1943, the ship was part of a convoy that was taking President Roosevelt to the high-level conferences at Cairo and Tehran. Somebody on board forgot to raise the anchor and the *Willie Dee* smacked into another destroyer as a result.

Tehran was frought with all kinds of security difficulties but these were coincidentally worsened by the activities of the *Willie Dee*. All four ships in the convoy initiated radio silence because of marauding Axis submarines. When an attack came, everybody manned battle stations and prepared for anti-sub manoeuvres. The whole thing was a false alarm – *Willie Dee* had accidentally dropped a depth charge off her stern, giving rise to the imminent attack panic.

The *Willie Dee* had to break off from the convoy for repairs as rough seas had flooded her engine room and had only just re-joined the others when near-disaster struck again. USS *Iowa* let off balloons for target practice, perhaps to impress FDR and *Willie Dee* joined in with torpedo drills. The combat crew forgot to remove the explosive charge from a missile headed right for the leader of the free world. Frantic attempts to signal *Iowa* went awry when the wrong message was sent – the incomprehensible 'WDP is breaking up'.

Roosevelt was sitting on deck in his wheelchair throughout this scare and reports exist claiming that his secret service bodyguards were firing at the incoming torpedo with their handguns! The torpedoes missed but that was hardly the point. The crew were arrested and court-martialled; Captain Dawson was sentenced to fourteen years hard labour, but the President used his power of commutation and all was forgiven.

Forgiven but not forgotten. Just in case *Willie Dee* was indeed a cursed ship, she was sent out of harm's way to the Aleutian Islands off Alaska – effectively in the middle of nowhere. On New Year's Eve, 1943, all was going well, with fireworks and merriment, when a sailor who had over-imbibed fired off a 5-inch gun, obliterating the flower garden of the local commandant.

In April 1945, *Willie Dee* took part in the battle of Okinawa. Bad enough that the US Navy had to contend with the mighty battleship, *Yamato*, and swarms of kamikaze (suicide) pilots, but the cursed ship contributed to the mayhem by accidentally straffing the USS *Luce*. The Pacific war was still raging on 10 June when a kamikaze pilot dove his plane directly at *Willie Dee*. He mistimed his attack and his aircraft ended up under the ship's keel, exploded and lifted *Willie Dee* out of the water. She keeled over and had to be abandoned although there were no casualties.

Bad luck? Gross incompetence? Deliberate sabotage? Or a genuine example of what superstitious sailors have known all along – a cursed ship. Whatever the situation, USS *William D Porter* received four battle stars for her service in the war.

THE DEVIL

!!

S ome Germans today, appalled by their country's recent past – or perhaps in denial over it – refer to Hitler as 'the man who made the Volkswagen'. In fact, although Hitler promised the 'people's car' as a cheap, efficient mode of transport for all civilians, it was not produced as such before the Reich was destroyed. In the 1940s, the KdF Wagen, as it was originally called, was used entirely by the armed forces. It was only after the war that the car was built on a massive scale, helping to rebuild the shattered German economy and becoming one of the world's most popular automobiles.

To some people, extolling the virtues of a machine built by a regime like the Nazis is abhorrent, but it does not end there. The industrial giant I.G. Farben, which claimed to make dyestuffs, was a corrupt cartel keeping its prices high and competition out. During the war it supplied the Wehrmacht with 85 per cent of its explosives and nearly all synthetic materials that kept the Nazi war machine rolling. Before the war, it had negotiated lucrative deals with the United States, Britain, France and Japan. Auschwitz, by 1944, was turning out oil and rubber products through the slave labour available there and elsewhere. In August 1945, the company's directors were put on trial for what amounted to war crimes but the eventual prosecution was dropped because the Americans realised that they needed German industrial muscle to counter the Cold War expansionist threat of Soviet Russia.

A subsidiary of Farben, Bayer, gave the world aspirin but it also produced Zyklon B, the cyanide capsules used to kill millions in the death camps. Prior to that, IBM had developed a punch-card system that allowed Nazi authorities to set up the equivalent of databases to hunt for the 'undesirables' that filled those camps. While the majority of German newspapers got out of the country as the war loomed, if not earlier, the Associated Press stayed, contributing to the Nazi propaganda of the *Volksischer Beobachter* and *Der Sturmer*. Krupp had been making German weapons since before there was a Germany (1871) – they willingly contributed to the Nazi war effort too. As did Hugo Boss, himself a passionate Nazi, who made SS uniforms using the camps' slave labour.

Sam Pivnik was a survivor of Auschwitz. Thirteen when the Germans invaded his native Poland, he survived the ghetto, two death camps, a death march and the mistaken bombing of the SS *Arcona* by the RAF in the spring of 1945. Years later, when John Kennedy was President of the United States, Pivnik saw a photograph of the man walking arm in arm with Werner von Braun, the Nazi who had devised the V2 missiles unleashed on Britain during the war. Von Braun was one of many former Nazis who had been embraced by the west because of his technological know-how, rather as many of today's international businesses once worked for Adolf Hitler and made a great deal of money out of him. 'A mass murderer,' said Pivnik, 'walking arm in arm with the leader of the free world.'

As President Kennedy might have said – 'Go figure.'

THE DEFECTOR

!!!

Martin James Monti was one of thousands of Americans who felt the draft. The United States might have dithered at the outbreak of the war in Europe, but the unprovoked attack by the Japanese at Pearl Harbor changed all that. Monti was from St Louis, Missouri and he joined the US Air Force as a cadet in 1943.

The next year found him as a second lieutenant based in Karachi, India, at a time when the whole of the sub-continent was still part of the British Empire. On 1 October 1944, Martin Monto suddenly went AWOL. He got to Cairo and on to Tripoli in Libya. The fighting here was long over, a combined force of British and American troops having forced Rommel's Afrika Korps off the coast. From there, Monti travelled north to Naples in the wake of the Allied armies who were closing in on Bologna. The Fascist dictator Benito Mussolini was on borrowed time by now. His ally Adolf Hitler advised him to pull back north of the River Po and the collapse of Italy and the fall of Mussolini were only weeks away.

Monti reached the 354th Air Service Squadron amidst the chaos and told them that he was a pilot from the 82nd air group. Oozing charm and confidence, he persuaded the 354th to let him test fly an F-5E Lightning, a version of the P-38 used for aerial reconnaissance and photography. He took off into the sun and literally vanished off the radar. Two hours later, in fact, he landed his hijacked aircraft near Milan in enemy territory. The Italian Social Republic was actually run by the Germans by this time and Monti, with an Italian name but mid-western American papers and accent, was taken prisoner.

So far, so odd, but it got odder. With the war's end, prisoners were released and Monti was back in Milan to re-join the American forces. But he was wearing an SS uniform, given to him, he said, by Italian partisans who had helped his escape. 1945-6 was a time of payback. Europe was in ruins, the Red Army was already squaring up to the West and there were, despite everybody's sense of exhaustion, scores to settle. Accordingly, Monti was court-martialled for desertion and the theft of a plane. He was sentenced to fifteen years in prison, but this was quashed as long as he re-enlisted as a private in the army. The media at the time had him down as an 'eager beaver' who longed for action rather than languishing in India, rather as hundreds of Americans had enlisted before December 1940 posing as Canadians to join the war effort.

But the case of Private Martin Monti did not quite add up. Facts were clouded with doubt; timelines did not fit. In 1947, the FBI turned up at Monti's army base in Florida and interviewed him. They discovered that he had made between ten and twenty broadcasts over the radio under the name Martin Wiethaupt, complaining about the Allied bombing of civilians. He had joined the SS as *Untersturmfuhrer* (second lieutenant); the uniform he had worn on his return to the fold was his own!

Monti faced trial again in 1949, but this time nobody was in a lenient mood. A huge case was presented involving witnesses who included former SS officers who offered testimony that the American had voluntarily enlisted in their ranks. To the astonishment of the prosecution, Monti pleaded guilty. He was sentenced to 25 years in prison and given a fine of $10,000 ($110,000 today). Two years later, he hit the headlines again, claiming that he was coerced into the guilty plea on advice from his counsel to avoid a death sentence. He was paroled in 1960 (so much for 25 years!) and lived quietly until his death in 2000.

What is weird about Monti's behaviour is the timing of the whole thing. There were any number of Italians and Germans in inter-war America who had doubts about where their loyalties lay. Some of them were openly Fascist but what could have motivated Monti to defect to the enemy so late in the war? It was common knowledge by October 1944 that the Italian war effort was in serious trouble. Even if Monti did not believe the British propaganda he would have read in Karachi, once he reached Naples he must have realised that Mussolini's Fascist state was dead in the water. What did he hope to achieve in the twilight of the war? If it was not defection, but some clever undercover plan of deception and subterfuge, again, what was the purpose? And why did Monti not explain himself? One of the mysteries lost to time.

THE DICTATOR OF BRISTOL

!!

Bristol is not known for its exotic wildlife. Sharing the honours with Liverpool as *the* part of western Britain, its wealth came from the slave-trade and the import of raw cotton. In the nineteenth century, it became forever linked with industrialisation and the ship-building genius of Isambard Kingdom Brunel.

But an even greater icon once graced the city and he can still be visited today. He is an adult male gorilla or silverback and peopled called him Alfred. He arrived at Bristol Zoo in 1930, at a time when few people had ever seen an animal like this. Used to endless wildlife programmes as we now are, thanks to television and the equally endless outpourings of David Attenborough, we are rather blasé about such things, but in the Thirties, Alfred was a sensation. Queues formed around the block to gawp at him in his cage and the press kept up a running commentary as he grew to maturity with a story on his 'first shave'!

When the Blitz hit London and other major cities in the autumn of 1940, a decision had to be made about zoo animals. They were expensive to keep at a time when money had to go to the war effort and the paying public were not inclined to risk queuing when death was raining from the skies. Many animals were put down. In the case of Alfred, however, he was neither destroyed nor evacuated, but remained stoically in his cage and became known as the dictator of Bristol, the city's answer to the human dictators who were bent on destroying Europe.

The soldiers stationed in the city loved him and postcards were sent to troops anxious for news from home, travelling as far as the United States, Australia and New Zealand. The fan club was not mutual, however – Alfred hated the thud of marching boots and let the passing troops know about it, snarling behind his bars and beating his considerable chest. By 1945, he was the official mascot of Bristol and when he died three years later, was stuffed and put on display in the city's museum and art gallery. In 1956, somebody broke in and stole Alfred, much to the horror of Bristolians. Whether through shame or the problem of keeping a seven foot animal somewhere under wraps where no one would notice him, he was returned three days later!

The case of the stolen dictator was finally solved in 2010 when one of the kidnappers made a deathbed confession. It was long overdue – the real age of the dictators had come to an end a long time before.

Richard Denham & M. J. Trow

THE DISAPPEARANCE
OF DOCTOR DEATH

!

A number of guards, commandants and especially doctors, have been given the grim sobriquet 'Dr. Death', but one who probably escaped retribution was Dr Aribert Heim, who became a physician in Austria's labour camp at Mauthausen in 1941.

Mauthausen was never an extermination camp, but it does hold the record of all concentration camps with 31, 318 executions logged in the *totenbuch* , the death book that the Nazis meticulously kept. Heim carried out gruesome operations on the inmates rather as Josef Mengele did at Auschwitz and literally held the power of life or death of thousands in his hands. By 1942, he had been transferred to Oulu in Finland, where his ghastly work continued. He was captured by the American army in March 1945 but soon released as no-one knew at that stage of his career at Mauthausen.

On 9 December 1946 twenty-three doctors, including one woman, were put on trial at Nuremberg charged with war crimes and crimes against humanity. Heim was not among them because, like so many other Nazis, he had slipped under the radar and was working as a gynaecologist somewhere in Germany.

In 1962, however, all that came to an end. The previous year there had been huge world-wide publicity as Adolf Eichmann, a leading player in the Holocaust, was caught, put on trial in Israel and executed. Everyone was looking harder at older German men with dodgy backgrounds and Heim thought it was time to vanish. He converted to Islam (totally at odds, of course, with Nazi doctrine) and took the name Tarek Hussein Farid. Despite the occasional letter to family and friends in Europe, Heim had, to all intents and purposes, disappeared and no-one knew exactly where he was.

Fast forward to 2007 when a book was published called *The Secret Executioner*. In it, the author, a former Israeli Air Force Colonel, Danny Baz, claimed that a clandestine organisation known as The Owl, tracked Heim down on the Californian island of Santa Catalina and executed him. The Simon Wiesenthal Foundation, set up after the war to hunt down such ex-Nazis has dismissed Baz's claim as fantasy.

ENEMY AT THE GATES

!!

If you have seen the excellent 2001 movie, *Enemy at the Gates*, you will be familiar with the broad brush strokes of the story. Stalingrad was a 'do or die' situation for Stalin's Red Army, as it was for von Paulus's Wehrmacht. It became the greatest killing ground in Russian history, and marked, perhaps, the beginning of the end for the Third Reich.

With modern, sophisticated weaponry and mass destruction from the air, the Second World War was not one in which personal heroics were common. But there were exceptions and in a killing ground like Stalingrad, the rivals stood out. Allowing for their different time and nationalities, they could have been Hector and Achilles of the ancient Greek world, from Homer's epic poem, *The Iliad*.

With the Wehrmacht was Erwin Konig, a world-class sniper who seemed to be everywhere in the grim street fighting in Stalingrad. Whenever a Russian soldier popped out of cover, even for seconds, he ran a huge risk of meeting one of Konig's bullets. His opposite number was Vasily Zaytsev, who became a 'hero of the Soviet Union' with his 225 kills, including 11 at Stalingrad. In the duel between these two, Zaytsev won, catching the weak sunglint on Konig's scope and shooting him in the head. Rather as heroes had done on battlefields for centuries, the Russian took Konig's scope and identity papers as souvenirs.

The problem with this apparently straightforward story is that Erwin Konig probably did not exist. He is not in any official Forces records (although it is true that many of these were destroyed at the end of the war); neither was there any sign of the daughter he was supposed to have; nor have the documents lifted from his body ever come to light. We only have the word of Vasily Zaytsev himself. And the Soviet authorities under Stalin, as before that time and since, have been all too eager to create good stories for propaganda purposes.

THE FALCON HAS LANDED

!!

'Sparrowhawks, Ma'am.' This was the famous solution suggested by the Duke of Wellington to Queen Victoria when she was worried about the hundreds of sparrows flying around the Crystal Palace in 1851 and the mess they would make on the fee-paying public below.

But birds of prey came to the county's rescue more recently. In the war years, the military and the secret service routinely used homing pigeons to carry messages from one part of the country to another, avoiding the use of telephones and radio frequencies. There was genuine concern that the enemy were doing the same and various pigeon centres were identified in Paris, Lille, Cherbourg and Angers.

So the British set up the Special Falconry Unit, using birds to intercept and kill 'enemy pigeons'. The Germans were also believed to have a Falcon Destruction Unit, a group of snipers poised to bring pigeon-hunting falcons down. No one seemed to be clear how a falcon could tell an enemy pigeon from 'one of ours' and the rate of 'friendly fire' must have been high.

If you are wondering why MI5 kept all this secret until it released the relevant files in 1999, perhaps it is because the whole notion is so laughable. Did these people not have a war to fight?

FIDO

!

In the often-confusing history of the Second World War, Fido was a French pilot who parachuted into England in July 1943. He was working for the German Secret Service (SD) and his mission was to steal a British plane and take it back to Germany. John Masterman, the head of the XX Committee, turned him and he never did fly back.

But Fido was something else too, nothing to do with the French aviator. It was all about the weather, which has done more to disrupt military operations than any enemy action in history. FIDO stood for Fog Investigation and Dispersal Operation or Fog, Intensive Dispersal Of (acronyms have a foaflore of their own!).

Britain had a particular dense fog that hovered over cities, which, combined with industrial output from hundreds of factory chimneys caused smog, a potentially lethal pollution that often caused large numbers of deaths. Londoners called them 'pea-soupers'. It was the RAF that was most concerned with this. Ground troops and even ships could cope with most fogs, but aircraft, before the advent of advanced navigation systems, flew by vision; a pilot had to see where he was going.

From 1943, a dispersal system had been worked out, spraying the air with calcium chloride using a 100ft pipe fitted with downward-pointing nozzles. As part of the country's efforts to stop the feared German invasion of 1940, Churchill's government set up the Petroleum Warfare Department with plans to set fire to Britain's beaches to deter landing. Two pipelines ran each side of a runway spraying out fuel. When an aircraft was due to land, men would run along the pipeline with flaming torches. The vapour ignited and the fog dispersed. The first test was not carried out until 1942, at Moody Down near Winchester and it was expensive, burning 450,000 litres of fuel an hour.

Fido's success was limited. It was a brave pilot who would land his aircraft between two walls of fire!

FLYING TANKS

!!!

As a weapon to replace the horse in battle, the tank was second to none. The name given as a cover for a bullet-proof armed vehicle running on its own caterpillar tracks in December 1915 was first used in warfare, at Cambrai two years later. Improved and modified as time went on, the tanks of the Second World War were battle-winners and spelt the end of conventional cavalry warfare.

Bearing in mind that aerial warfare also came of age in the twentieth century, ideas were being bandied about of machines combining the two - a 'flying' tank that could be dropped from the sky into the middle of a battle. The most highly developed form was Russia's Antonov A-40, designed by Oleg Antonov, which, theoretically, worked!

Existing armoured vehicles, especially jeeps, were routinely dropped by parachutes from aircraft, especially by the SAS and other commando units who operated behind enemy lines. The problem was that such machinery was often damaged on impact with the ground and the crews dropped moments later would often be a long distance from their vehicles.

Antonov's wings were a work of genius, linked to the turret, so that the tank commander could tilt them in the same way that he turned the vehicle left or right. In the end, it was decided that, tactically, the expensive flying tank was not much of an improvement on the conventional type, which would free up the necessity of cargo aircraft/bombers that could be used for other things.

THE GAULEITER OF THE BAHAMAS

!!!

In the 1930s, Britain had mixed views on Adolf Hitler and the Nazi party. On the one hand, wily old politicians like David Lloyd George, a former prime minister, were impressed by the Führer and the economic 'miracle' he was presiding over in war-torn Germany. Some members of the House of Lords, such as Brockett and Londonderry were, to say the least, non-comital about Nazi policies. Prominent politicians like Lord Halifax at the Foreign Office, did not want to bomb the Ruhr, once the war had begun, because it was private property! Still others, like the charismatic MP Oswald Moseley and the dour Admiral Barry Domville, were openly Fascist, praising both Hitler and Mussolini as saviours of their respective countries. Men like Winston Churchill, demonising these leaders as tin-pot dictators, were very few and far between, 'in the wilderness' on the fringes of events.

The position of the Royal Family was also surprisingly dubious. By definition,the Windsors had, until 1914, been the Battenbergs – the line of royal descent had been bound with Germany since the arrival of Geroge I in 1714 – and many of the titled courtiers around the king were either pro-German (such as the Duke of Buccleuch) or anti-war, or both. Even as late as February 1940, by which time the war had been raging for six months, Buccleuch was writing that the war would 'play into the hands of Soviet Russia, Jews and Americans'.

The abdication crisis of 1936 threw a spanner into the royal works. Obsessed with protocol and tradition, the rest of 'the firm' were appalled when Edward, Prince of Wales, a tennis-playing and not very bright playboy, fell in love with Wallis Simpson, an American divorcee. On all counts she was unsuitable as a future queen. She was divorced (which the Church of England could not countenance). She was a commoner with not even noble, yet alone royal blood. *And* she was American. Despite the fact that the Americans had fought with Britain in the First World War, there was no 'special relationship' then; there had been more wars against them than with them. But 'Eddie Windsor' would not be swayed. Determined to marry Simpson, he made an emotional plea-cum-explanation over the radio to his astonished people and abandoned the throne, passing it to his younger brother who became George VI. There is little doubt from what we know, that George's wife, Elizabeth (still known, affectionately in Britain as 'the queen mother') was pro-appeasement and a fan of both Neville Chamberlain, the prime minister, and Lord Halifax. It is likely that the new king was too.

Edward VIII had abdicated on 10 December, making his the shortest reign since that of Edward V in the fifteenth century. He and Mrs Simpson (now the Duke and Duchess of Windsor) moved to Austria and France where they were married and spent some time in Portugal where there was a ludicrous plan, run by the spymaster Walter Schellenberg, to coax the ex-monarch over to the German side. Nothing came of it and the Windsors were only delayed for a few hours. In 1937 Edward was the official guest of the Führer in Berlin and photographs of the pair, smiling and shaking hands, were beamed around the world.

In the end, probably to keep him out of harm's way, Churchill sent the Duke to the Bahamas as governor of the island. He had returned to Britain shortly before war began, but his position was thought to be untenable.

Was Edward, Duke of Windsor, a Nazi? Probably not, but there are many things relating to the Second World War, the Royal Family, and senior politicians, which are not yet – and perhaps never will be – in the public domain. The jury is still out. As Edward once said to Patrick Balfour 'I never thought Hitler was such a bad chap.' How enigmatic is that?

THE GOLD OF THE NORTH

!

Amber is a fossil resin from extinct coniferous trees and is found mostly in the clays of the Oligosene system. It is particularly common in Eastern Germany and was known in the eighteenth century as the gold of the north. An entire chamber, lined and decorated with amber, was built in Prussia in 1701 by Andreas Schlüter to enhance the Charlottenburg Palace in Berlin nearly two centuries before Germany came into existence.

The 'eighth wonder of the world' was visited by the Russian Tsar Peter the Great in 1716. Peter was one of the great reforming rulers of Russia, bringing his backward, almost medieval kingdom kicking and screaming into modernity. Frederick Wilhelm of Prussia would much rather have the man as an ally than an enemy and gave him the amber chamber as a gift. It was deconstructed, slab by slab, and rebuilt in the Catherine Palace, St Petersburg.

Fast forward to June 1941. Operation Barbarossa was the end result of Hitler's expansionist foreign policy in the east. He had recently built an alliance with Stalin's Soviet Union in order to destroy Poland, but that objective achieved, it was time to achieve his *lebensraum* (living space) further east. St. Petersburg was now Leningrad, renamed in honour of the father of the Soviet State and Hitler, who saw himself as an art connoisseur, wanted the amber room to come home to Germany.

Once again it was dismantled and reconstructed, this time in Koningsberg Castle and was on public display for two years. In 1945, however, the intense Allied bombing of Germany, by British and American aircraft, day and night, saw the medieval fortress collapse into rubble. And with it, the amber room vanished.

One man obsessed with what happened to it was General Kuchumov. It was under his watch that the room had been taken from Leningrad four years earlier and he was not about to let it happen again. But the general had no luck. There was no obvious signs of amber in the ruins of Koningsberg, so a host of conspiracy theories emerged. Some claimed the whole edifice had been smuggled on board the Wilhelm Gustaff, a German merchantship that was sunk with a huge loss of life in 1945. Others believed that the room lay in the myriad secret tunnels underneath Koningsberg Castle. Yet more pointed to Czech salt mines and the existence of the fabulous room under some musky lagoon. When the Soviet authorities destroyed the ruins of Konigsberg in 1968 the amber room vanished forever.

But not quite. Two men who, like Kuchumov, became obsessed with the search for the room died in suspicious circumstances. Georg Stein, an ex-German soldier and historian spent years investigating the chamber's disappearance. He was murdered by disembowelling in 1987. General Yuri Gusev, head of Russia's Foreign Intelligence Unit, was looking for it also when he was killed in a suspicious car crash in 1992.

Was the truth simply that Stalin's own bombers, rather than those of the Allies, had destroyed the amber room? The Soviet Union, before its collapse in the 90s, was all about reputation and saving face. Is that why Stein and Gusev died?

If you want to see the amber chamber today, you can. In 1979 it was reconstructed from original drawings and photographs in the Catherine Palace and the room officially opened in 2003.

GUSTAV SIEGFRIED EINS

!!!

Intelligence and communication were war-winners between 1939 and 1945. The British Secret Intelligence Service (SIS) began to use 'wireless' in 1938 and during the war there were 48 clandestine shortwave radio stations in Britain, broadcasting in 14 languages. The first, in May 1940, was codenamed G1 and was in response to a similar set-up in Berlin run by Josef Goebbels' Ministry of Propaganda and Enlightenment, which ran stations like Radio Caledonia, Welsh National Radio and, ironically, Christian Peace Movement.

The first of the Germans to front the British G1 service was Dr Carl Spiecker, an anti-Nazi who had earlier operated against the Reich from Paris. But the real brains behind the broadcasting network was 'Tom' Sefton Delmer (whose name was actually Dennis), an Australian journalist brought up in Germany. His German was impeccable and he coined the term 'black' propaganda for subversive deception to fool the enemy. Delmer himself described the difference between white and black propaganda, saying it was a bit like spitting in a German's soup before shouting 'Heil Hitler!'

GS1 (Gustav Siegfried Eins) was a right-wing station that used (for the time) bad language and appeared to stand one hundred per cent behind the Fuhrer. As Delmer wrote to his boss, Leonard Ingrams, 'We want to spread disruptive and disturbing news among the Germans which will induce them to distrust their government and disobey it.' GS1's first broadcast, two weeks after the event, covered Rudolf Hess's bizarre flight to Scotland, which was being officially ignored by Churchill's government. To add to its authenticity, Delmer hired a German actor and crime writer, Peter Seckelmann, to voice *Der Chef* (Hitler's nickname among his staff in the 1930s) and a journalist, Johannes Reinholz, as his heel-clicking Number Two. If it all sounds like an episode of the 1980s sitcom *'Allo! 'Allo!*, we have to remember that the 1940s was a different decade and people in desperate, terrifying situations relied on radio – *any* radio at times – as a lifeline. Seckelmann went to live with Delmer and his wife at The Rookery in Aspley Guise within a stone's throw of the secret code and cypher school at Bletchley Park. *Der Chef* was supposed to be an old-school German, disapproving of the hypocrisy and rumoured degeneracy of the Nazi elite. The whole thing was carefully orchestrated to sound like a private conversation in a pub rather than a broadcast to potential thousands.

With its outspoken attacks on 'that flat-footed bastard of a drunken old cigar-smoking Jew, Churchill', the Gestapo believed that Gustav Siegfried Eins was a genuine station and tried to work out what the name itself meant.

In the end, the station closed, after over 700 broadcasts, because Sefton Delmer went too far. In one programme, *Der Chef* described witnessing an orgy. The script got to the desk of Sir Stafford Cripps, who was so appalled by the idea that he wrote to Anthony Eden, the Foreign Secretary, on 12 June 1942, that he objected to 'such filth being allowed to go out of this country. If this is the sort of thing needed to win the war, I'd rather lose it!'

Cripps' heart was in the right place, but he clearly had no grasp of black propaganda at all. Gustav Siegfried Eins came to an abrupt end on 11 November 1943 when the Gestapo were heard storming the station, screaming at *Der Chef*, 'I've finally caught you, you pig!' before killing him in a crescendo of machine-gun fire. The sound engineer handling the woofers and tweeters spoke no German and misunderstood his cue, playing the massacre twice in a row.

Gustav Siegfried Eins – so good, they shot it twice!

TO HELL AND BACK

!!

What do you have to do to get your name in a book? *Chambers Biographical Dictionary* (1990 edition) has four Murphies. One was a nineteenth century Irish playwright; another is an Australian dancer; a third was an American doctor and the fourth is Eddie, the black American 'comic performer'. But, bizarrely, the most famous Murphy of them all is not included. He was a genuine hero of the Second World War and arguably accomplished more in his brief military career than all of *Chumber's* other Murphies put together.

Audie Murphy was born in a Texas farming community, one of twelve children. The family was broken up when Audie's father abandoned them and his mother died when the boy was sixteen. With his fresh, freckled face and clear blue eyes, he went to join the US Marines in 1942 but at 5ft 5in he was too short. He must have 'walked tall' (as he did in innumerable Fifties Westerns later) as the army *did* take him. He claimed to be eighteen, which he was not, and saw action in North Africa, Italy (the battle of Anzio and the liberation of Rome) and the south of France.

His greatest moment came on 26 July 1945 near Holtwihr in eastern France. His unit was attacked by six panzers and a force of 250 men. The Americans fell back, but not Murphy. He clambered into a blazing tank and blasted away with a machine gun, killing fifty of the enemy in a hail of bullets. When his unit had time to reform, Murphy, bleeding from wounds in both legs and out of ammunition, attacked with them.

By the end of the war, Murphy was only 21 years old, but he had won every single medal awarded to American soldiers, including the coveted purple heart, the highest accolade for a wounded man's gallantry in the field. Hollywood could not leave this man alone. Like James Stewart, Errol Flynn and Glenn Ford who also saw active service, Murphy was the stuff of legend before he ever put on a ten-gallon hat! He starred in over forty feature films, mostly Westerns, in a simplistic era when the good guy in the white hat always got the girl and beat the baddie.

In reality, the heart-throb who looked like the boy next door suffered from post traumatic stress disorder as a result of his wartime experiences. Few people recognized the condition, believing it to be shell-shock only experienced in the trenches of the First World War. Murphy highlighted the problem and brought it to the public's attention for perhaps the first time. In his darkest moments, which no one outside a chosen few ever knew about, he suffered from insomnia and nightmares and slept with a loaded pistol under his pillow.

Audie Murphy was killed in a plane crash in Virginia in 1971 and was buried with full military honours in Arlington National Cemetery. It is one of the most commonly visited war graves.

In 1955, Hollywood made a movie called *To Hell and Back* based on the man's 1949 autobiography. Who played him? Audie Murphy.

HIBAKUSHA

!

'Now I am become Death' says the Hindu Holy book, the Bhagavad-Gita, 'The Destroyer of Worlds'. Dr. Robert Oppenheimer, one of the leading physicists behind America's atomic bomb programme, the Manhattan Project, quoted this to describe the impact of the weapon he had helped to create

On 6 August 1945, Colonel Paul Tibbets of the United States Air Force flew his B-29 Superfortress, Enola Gay, over the Japanese city of Hiroshima and dropped a uranium fission bomb equivalent to 20,000 tons of TNT. Sixty percent of the city was flattened (later aerial photographs show a ghostly wasteland) and there were 80,000 dead in minutes. Worse destruction was caused by the bombing of Tokyo in March, but nothing had the dramatic impact of Hiroshima. For a single plane to cause so much devastation was unbelievable. Three days later, Nagasaki received the same treatment, using a more advanced plutonium bomb. The casualties were about half those of Hiroshima. Despite some opposition from his High Command, Emperor Hirohito surrendered. In a broadcast to his people over Japanese radio, he said 'We have resolved to endure the unendurable and suffer what is insufferable.'

Those who suffered most were the hibakusha, literally, 'a person affected by a bomb'. Robert Louis Stevenson had no idea how right he was when he wrote in the boys' adventure story, *Treasure Island*, 'Them's that die will be the lucky ones'. The bombs of August caused horrendous physical and mental problems for the survivors. A total of about a quarter of a million died from radiation sickness as well as the bombs themselves and various forms of cancer are linked to this.

What is grim is that the hibakusha were despised and discriminated against by the Japanese themselves. They were not given jobs in the years ahead. Would-be in laws objected to their sons' and daughters' marriage partners in case radiation were to be passed on to succeeding generations. To the West, Japanese culture had always appeared odd, but the psychological effects of being the only country in the world to have suffered the atom bomb are still on-going.

It even finds its way into popular sci-fi culture today. Godzilla is a monster bent on destruction, smashing its way through cities with ease. And Godzilla was created as a result of nuclear warfare. If you are a fan of horror films, you will almost certainly have heard a piece of music linked to all this. Written by the Polish composer Krzysztof Penderecki in 1960, it is called 'Threnody to the Victims of Hiroshima'.

HITLER'S WOMEN

!!

In the carefully constructed propaganda surrounding Adolf Hitler, beautiful girls and blond, blue-eyed children were always caught by the camera at the front of the crowd, cheering wildly and beaming adoringly at their Fuhrer. To the girls, he was 'der schone Adolf' (handsome Adolf). It was all part of the cult of leadership adopted by other dictators like Mussolini and Stalin; but nobody did it better than the Nazis.

Hitler's private life was very diffcrent however. Most people today see the man as the epitome of evil, a megalomaniac with no redeeming features, a sociopath who was utterly immune to other people's suffering. While all this is true, it does not begin to plumb the depths of his psychosis and leaves us guessing about his sexuality.

There were those who hinted that the young Adolf was homosexual and that one of his lovers was Rudolf Hess, his 'Hesserl', who was one of his earliest supporters. There is no evidence of this and by virtue of what he did, a balanced, rational approach to Hitler's psyche is probably not possible. He certainly adored his mother, the plodding, religiously inclined Klara Poelzl and looked like her. He was her favourite child – 'mother's darling' – but he let her down by not joining the priesthood as she had hoped but trying to become an artist instead.

There were four women rumoured to have been romantically linked with Hitler. The first was Maria Reiter, known as Mimi, who attempted suicide in 1928 when the

Nazi party had been reborn with Hitler as its leader and the bully-boys of Ernst Röhm's SA still dominated. Maria was a 16-year-old shop assistant from Oberzalzberg and Hitler was thirty seven. He promised to marry her but his mission for Germany got in the way. Depressed and lonely, she tried to hang herself but her brother-in-law cut her down in the nick of time. She went on to marry SS Hauptsturmfuhrer Georg Kubisch who was killed at Dunkirk in May 1940. Mimi told her story to *Stern* magazine in 1959 and she died in 1992.

It was the second relationship, however, that shone a spotlight on the future Fuhrer's private life. In 1931, Hitler was still only the leader of a fringe political party regarded as a joke by most Germans. On 19 September of that year, his niece, Geli Raubal, was found dead in Hitler's apartment at 16 Prinzregentenplatz in Munich. She had shot herself with Hitler's pistol. The image that the Nazi leader had carefully cultivated was that of a 'man alone', wedded to the concept of a German revival after the disaster of the First World War; his private life was on hold because Germany must come first. Yet here was a possible mistress so unhappy with the new messiah that she had killed herself. Geli had been seeing Hitler's chauffeur-bodyguard, Emil Maurice and 'Uncle Adolf' was furious, flying into one of his legendary rages. The jury is still out on exactly what the Hitler-Raubal relationship was, but it may very well have been sexual. He certainly had a private shrine to the girl in his Munich flat, as witnessed by the film-maker Leni Riefenstahl, with flowers around a bust of her. It took him months to recover from his loss.

Very different was Unity Mitford. One of a nightmarish brood of daughters of David Freemantle-Mitford, 2nd Baron Redesdale, the fact that her middle name was Valkyrie gave a hint as to her Teutonic leanings. Tall, blonde and just as eccentric as her father, she drifted to Munich in 1933, the year that Hitler took power, and became a much-photographed member of his circle. She fell madly (how else?) in love with him and probably saw herself as Frau Fuhrer. Whereas the Nazis deliberately excluded women from serious political discussion, Unity spoke loudly, usually extolling the virtues of Britain, at every gathering she went to. On the day that Neville Chamberlain's Britain declared war on Germany, Unity sat on a bench in the appropriately named Englischer Garten in Munich and put a bullet in her head. The calibre was small, however, and she did not die. Hitler sent his best doctors to treat her and she was sent home via Switzerland. She died in 1948, never having recovered from her suicide attempt, still declaring her love for the man who had murdered six million Jews.

Eva Braun never discussed politics, which may be why she lasted so relatively long. The daughter of a Munich teacher, she was tall and athletic, without much of a brain and little in the way of ambition. She was a semi-professional dancer, but shy and quiet, in many ways the perfect partner for a politician who veered towards the autocratic. 'A highly intellectual man,' he once said, 'should have a primitive and stupid woman. Imagine if I had a woman to interfere with my work.' Both Goebbels and Goering introduced Hitler to Nordic beauties but the Fuhrer was not interested. Eva, known to her servants as 'E.B.', stayed in the background at Berchtesgaden, keeping out of the way while Hitler talked politics with the great and not so good of Nazi Germany. Not until 1943 was she allowed to go to Berlin and they would never be seen together in public. He treated her abysmally, taking her for granted and she too, like the other three women in Hitler's life, attempted suicide.

And she finally succeeded in typically Wagnerian style. Hiding in the bunker under the streets of Berlin while Russian shells devastated the streets, Hitler married Eva Braun and they committed suicide together. On that last day when a servant referred to Eva with the usual 'grädiges fräulein' (gracious lady) she smiled and said, 'You may now safely call me grädiges Frau!' (In other words, Mrs Hitler). Although details are unclear, Hitler probably shot himself in the head and Eva swallowed poison.

All four women linked with the Fuhrer attempted suicide. Why? The American Office of Strategic Services (OSS), forerunner of the CIA, carried out a study of the dictator while he was still alive and came to the conclusion that he was an impotent homosexual with a faeces fixation. But then, to paraphrase someone else in a rather different context, 'they would, wouldn't they?'

I LOVE LUCY

!!

Lucille Desirée Ball was a dizzy, red-headed comedienne who was a child model and chorus girl before gravitating to B-feature movies and television. Between 1951 and 1973, she was a hit in a variety of shows, all featuring her own effervescent character with or without her straight man, first husband Desi Arnaz.

In 1942, then in her early thirties, Lucy was driving home from the MGM film lot in Hollywood where she was working on the movie *Du Barry is a Lady*. It was then that she started hearing music. Her car had a radio but it was not switched on and she realised to her horror that the sound was coming from her mouth. For a while, she kept the information to herself, believing she might be going mad. In the end, she told her story to a man who, on the big screen at least, could be guaranteed to keep a secret – the 'silent' comedian, Buster Keaton. Keaton had an explanation – he had a friend with a similar problem and it was caused by fillings in the teeth.

The next time Lucy heard the sounds, she was again alone in her car, but the sound was not music, it was morse code. By now, thoroughly unnerved, she told her bosses at MGM and they, equally alarmed, passed the whole thing over to the FBI. The Federal Bureau of Investigation was (and is) responsible for law enforcement in the United States, but during the war, its remit included counter-espionage and sabotage. As a result of their enquiries, the Feds uncovered a Japanese spy ring and several arrests followed.

Is all this true? Or does it belong in the Boston Herald Rumor Clinic category? Scientifically it is just about feasible that the metal in a tooth cavity could pick up a radio wave, but whether it did and whether the FBI were able to carry out the work they did, remains conjecture.

I WAS HITLER'S MAID

!!!

Pauline Kohler was one of an unknown number of Germans who was overheard making a disparaging remark about the Fuhrer. Such paranoia was not confined to Nazi Germany – in Britain too, defeatist comments and gripes about Churchill landed people in gaol.

In the Third Reich, however, punishments were harsher and Pauline found herself interrogated, tied to a chair naked, by the Gestapo, before being sent to Buchenwald, the camp near Weimar. Even as early as 1940, the place was notorious for its routine torture of prisoners and the grim work carried out in the camp's munitions factory.

Pauline survived and ended up working as a maid for a Gestapo officer, who abused her on a daily basis before his wife intervened, pulling strings and got the girl a job as a domestic at the Berghof, Hitler's idyllic retreat in the Bavarian mountains, near Salzburg.

To her horror, she found that the Führer was every bit the monster she had heard recent mutterings about. There was a 'rape dungeon' in the house's cellar and the whole place was littered with sadistic pornography. High-ranking Nazis were frequent visitors.

None of this surprised Hitler's enemies, inside Germany and elsewhere. The trouble was, it was all fiction. Pauline Kohler wrote '*I was Hitler's Maid* (retitled '*The Woman Who Lived in Hitler's House*' for the American market) in 1940. The book was an immediate best seller translated into seven languages, even Chinese! *Hitler's Maid* is an excellent example of black propaganda and the real author was probably Robert Collier, who rattled the whole sordid nonsense off on an upright typewriter in just two weeks. Pauline's face, on the original cover of the book, the terrified victim and martyr, is actually a photo-edit of four women put together!

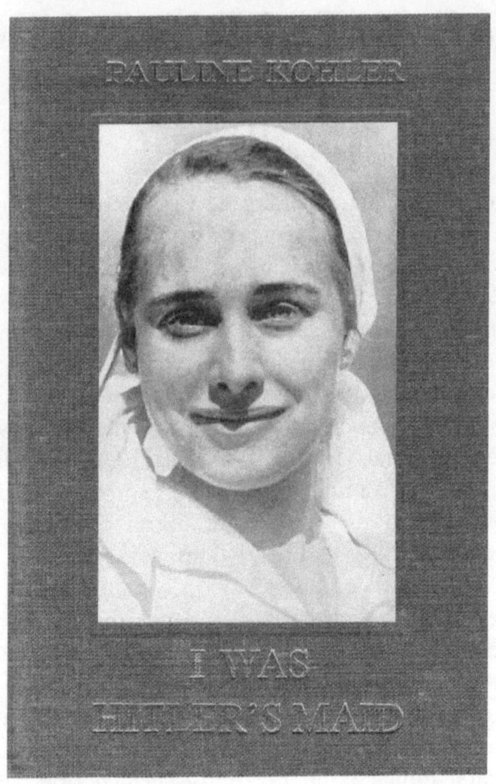

ICE CREAM

!

Despite various attempts by the Italians and the Arabs to claim to have developed ice cream as an exotic dish, no one did it like the Americans. The Knickerbocker Glory was named after a Dutch family who settled in the States, the name itself being hijacked by Washington Irving for a stage comedy. Rocky Road was developed by William Dreyer as an attempt to console those who lost money in the Wall Street 'crash' of 1929. The 'Doughboys' of 1917-18 had ice cream as part of their staple diet, while their 'Tommy' comrades in Britain only ever regarded it as a seaside treat in the height of summer.

In the Second World War, the GIs fighting their way east through the forest of the Ardennes made ice cream in their helmets using snow and the chocolate bars they were given in their rations. In the air, the crews of B-52s took their own ice cream with them, in the freezing cold compartments of the rear-gunners. At altitudes of 15-18,000 feet, custard froze and was churned by a combination of engine vibration and turbulence to make a delicious concoction.

Even in the Pacific, the US army were well provided with the stuff in their desperate battles with the Japanese. An ice cream barge in the South Pacific produced 38 litres of the stuff every seven minutes and could store up to 7,600 litres.

And in the British war effort? Because of the internment of so many Italians under Defence Regulation 18B, ice cream parlours all but disappeared. Those not interned had to make do with carrots on lolly sticks!

IF DAY

!!!

Fur traders settled along the Red River in Canada before 1763 and the area was protected by the army at Fort Garry. A settlement quickly grew up around it and it became Winnipeg city in 1879, growing into a fine mini-metropolis as befits the capital of Manitoba. It has churches, schools, hospitals, lumber yards and factories, a thriving and successful icon of western knowhow and ambition.

Then, at 5.30am on 19 February 1942, all that came to an end. Air raid sirens wailed in the darkness of the morning, the radio crackled with the shocking news that the Wehrmacht were entering the town and nearly 4000 of them, helmeted and jackbooted, strutted up the streets and squares, bringing terror in their wake. The local garrison at Fort Garry fought back, but they were hopelessly outnumbered and by 9.30am the maple-leaf flag over the fort was lowered and a swastika ran up the ropes instead.

Books were dragged out of the library and burned in the street, exactly as the Nazis had done in Germany when they seized power. Posters were slapped up on walls and lamp posts telling the locals what they could and could not do. Anyone failing to obey would face harsh reprisals. In the shops Reichmarks were already replacing dollars at the payment counters.

The odd thing about all this, horrified observers noticed, was that there was no devastation. They had heard the siren, but they had not heard – or seen – aircraft. They had heard the guns, but no buildings were lacerated by shrapnel; no glass had been broken. Above all, there were newsreel cameras everywhere, recording it all for posterity.

Enter the German High Command in the form of J.D. Perrin, at the Great Winnipeg Victory home Corporation. The whole thing was a stunt using film extras and cobbled together uniforms, to be shown in cinemas across Canada exactly what to expect if Canada did not take its responsibility to the war effort seriously. An astonishing $3million was raised in war bonds.

And the day's casualties after all the sound and fury of slaughter? A soldier sprained his ankle, and a woman burnt her hand making toast in the morning's blackout!

KNITTING FOR ENGLAND

!

'Genevieve' was one of that brave little band of female agents parachuted behind enemy lines by SOE, the Special Operations Executive set up by Churchill to 'set Europe aflame'. Her real name was Phyllis Latour Doyle and she used the knitting skills she had learned as a girl to create secret codes. Such messages took about thirty minutes to send, so Phyllis kept on the move, sending a total of 135 in the runup to D-Day to keep the Allies informed of German troop movements.

The Belgians specialised in knitters in their Resistance organisations. Who would suspect a granny sitting on a park bench, clacking away with a pair of needles? Knitting is actually a binary system, with easily identifiable v (a knit stitch) or o (a purl) as the two symbols. Either a knitting pattern or the finished garment can easily be read by an expert. Everybody was at it – in the States, Elizabeth Beatty knitted codes for communists in the Soviet Union until 1945. In Britain, knitting patterns were banned in the post in case they carried secret codes.

Knitting for troops at the front, however, was a well-established support. Wives and mothers had been doing this for generations and governments encouraged it. As one American poster put it – 'Remember Pearl Harbor, Purl Harder!'

THE LITTLE DUTCH GIRLS

!

The Netherlands has a long feisty history in European politics. Fighting against the might of Spain for their beginnings in the sixteenth century, they emerged as a leading maritime nation a century later, going head to head with Britain for control of the northern fishing market. In the First World War, however, they remained neutral, appalled at the ease with which the Kaiser's army swept through 'neutral' Belgium just miles to the south.

On 10 May 1940, despite being officially neutral again, the Netherlands found themselves facing the German blitzkrieg, far more terrifying than the Kaiser's attack in 1914. This was *Case Yellow*, the code name for a simultaneous attack on the Netherlands, Belgium, Luxembourg and France. At last, the West could now believe that the 'phoney war' was over. Thirty divisions of German Army Group B under General Fedor von Bock swept the northern end of the Siegfried Line and made for the coast, Amsterdam and the Hague.

Five days later, it was all over. Holland has low-lying marshland that could slow an invasion, but had no mountain ranges or deep forests and it was no contest. Compared with other occupations by the Nazis, the German impact om the Netherlands was measured and mild, a 'velvet glove' approach all too rare in the 1940s.

The Oversteegen family knew about Nazi atrocities

elsewhere. The war had been raging in the east for eight months by now and rumours had been coming out of Germany itself for years. Trijn, the mother, was a Communist who had already welcomed dissidents fleeing from the Reich, Jews and homosexuals among them. The Dutch Resistance approached her for support and her teenaged daughters, Freddie and Truus, readily agreed.

Often wearing their old school uniforms, the sisters flirted with local Wehrmacht units, young men who missed their girlfriends and wives and could be seduced fairly easily. On one occasion, Truus went for a walk in the woods with an SS officer and rather than the slap and tickle he expected, he met members of the Resistance, who shot him! The girls almost certainly killed men themselves, shooting soldiers as they cycled passed on their bikes. At other times, they sheltered Jewish children, not much younger than they were, keeping them away from the trains that were taking them for 'resettlement' in the east.

Children are often caught up in war situations and the danger was very real. One of their cell, Hannie Schaft, known to the Germans as 'the girl with the red hair' was caught and executed by Dutch Nazis three weeks before the war ended.

Both Oversteegen girls survived and were officially decorated by the Dutch government in 2014. Truus died two years later and Freddie in 2018. What they had done and what they had seen went to their graves with them.

THE MAD COLONEL

!!

A conflict like the Second World War throws up heroes and heroines of all shapes and sizes, but few stand taller than Lt Col Robert Blaire Mayne, DSO, known universally as 'Paddy'. It was only his select friends, however, who called him that to his face, because he was a huge, unpredictable Irishman and nobody could be sure exactly what he would do next. His favourite song was the German import *Lili Marlene*, and the First Special Air Service, of which he was colonel, often sang it into the small hours at their celebrated parties, in which 'conspicuous amounts' of liquor were consumed.

1SAS had its origins with the Long Range Desert group, a bunch of maverick commandos fighting in North Africa. Physically tough and highly-trained commandos, they and their naval equivalent – the Special Boat Services – had a reputation second to none for getting things done. They were all volunteers and the thought of being returned to their original units was the worst shame that could befall any of them.

His men worshipped Paddy Mayne, whether he was singing in the Mess, tackling them hard in a game of rugger or broadcasting over the camp radio in the days after D-Day when the SAS were scattered behind enemy lines. But he impressed them most when he led from the front, as he always did, facing every danger that the Wehrmacht could throw at them. Six foot three, a boxer and a former Irish rugby international, the colonel had made his name in North

Africa before launching a series of spectacular raids on enemy airfields. He was determined, as many commanders were not, never to lose a man in the field. He slept in the open wherever he could and disliked the 'indoors' atmosphere of the officers' Mess. He had an air of carelessness about him and a fighter's instinct for danger. He missed nothing. A first class marksman, his eagle eyes were everywhere. He was known to be kind and generous over army infringements, but to him, the one unforgiveable sin was a man not wearing his beret straight. The sloppy wearer of the headgear at an angle was looking for trouble.

Perhaps Mayne's most dazzling exploit was while he was operating in conjunction with the Long Range Desert Group in North Africa. The unit launched a daring attack on the airfield of Sidi Haneish, thirty miles south of Mersa Matruh, a base for Stuka divebombers. The SAS, under David Stirling, went in, literally with all guns blazing, hitting the airfield at 1.30am. As luck would have it, a plane coming in at that moment lit up the whole strip and gave the SAS a spotlight for their targets. They drove their jeeps between the parked aircraft, shredding them with Vickers machinegun fire.

Paddy Mayne, having sprinted across open ground to plant a bomb under the wing of a Heinkel III and see it blow sky high, dashed into an outbuilding just as drunken Luftwaffe pilots were tumbling out of bed to see what the commotion was. Mayne opened up with his Bren gun and may have been responsible for more kills that day than any of the airborne aces of the war! Afterwards, with the airfield destroyed and daylight dawning, Medical officer Malcolm Playdell saw Mayne lolling in the back of a jeep reading a paperback. His comment on the raid? 'Oh, it was quite good craic!'

For several men of the SAS, the end of the war brought boredom and bitterness. Mayne himself drove his Riley sports car into a parked lorry after a few pints too many, in December 1955.

There is one curious story about him that has never

been explained. For reasons unknown, he despised the broadcaster Richard Dimbleby who reported, for example, on the death camps discovered by the Allies in the autumn of 1944 and early 1945. He threatened to kill him on more than one occasion. Had he been serious and had he done so, how different the BBC of the post war world would have been!

THE MAD HATTER

!!!

Among the 'fellow travellers of the Right' who championed the cause of Fascism in the 1930s, James Larratt Battersby stands out. His family were successful hat makers at a time when stylish headgear was an essential fashion accessory for both sexes. The family produced 12,000 hats a week and employed over 1,000 people.

The Russian Revolution of 1917, based on the Communist doctrine of Karl Marx, had spread its ideas beyond the confines of the Soviet Union and Fascism had grown up as a rival orthodoxy. Whereas Britain was known for its tolerant, middle-of-the-road politics, countries like Germany, Italy, Spain and to a lesser extent, France, became caught up in the extremism of the age.

James Battersby joined the British Union of Fascists, the pro-Mussolini and pro-Hitler movement founded by Oswald Mosley, a prominent politician disillusioned by the spinelessness of the government of the day. Battersby ran the Stockport branch of the party, which became increasingly unpopular over its attitude towards Jews and, after September 1939, its support of the enemy. Along with several others, Battersby was interred at Camp 020, Latchmere House, under Regulation 18B which dealt with espionage and aliens.

He was eventually moved to the Isle of Man where he met Thomas Guillame St. Barbe Baker who believed that Hitler was the reincarnation of Jesus Christ. This was not too surprising – after all, millions of Germans saw him in the same light. In 1943 Battersby and Baker set up the legion of

Christian Reformers Unity, a manifesto (along the lines of Hitler's *Mein Kampf*) which placed the Führer as God's champion against the devil.

After the war, as a shattered country tried to get back to normality, the deranged pair set up Kingdom House in seventeenth century premises at Peworth, Sussex, donated by another fellow traveller, the barrister W.G. Barlow. Here, a commune of Fascists held forth. They bought a bust of their dead Fuhrer from an auction and draped the building with swastikas. In 1952 Battersby did his best to interrupt the memorial service at the Cenotaph in Whitehall, ranting his Fascist nonsense before being arrested. The previous year he had published *The Holy Book and Testament of Adolf Hitler*, not exactly a runaway best seller.

In 1955 James Battersby killed himself by jumping from the Mersey ferry. His head was taken off by the paddles. In the suicide note he sent to a newspaper beforehand, he wrote 'My work here is complete. I follow the Fuhrer to glory and eternity. Through the sacrifice of the Aryan martyrs our world victory is assured. Heil Hitler.'

MEN IN HIGH CASTLES

!!

The Man in the High Castle is an American television series whose dystopian plot is that the Germans and the Japanese won the Second World War and what happens in the United States as a result. There have been a number of movies and novels on this theme since the war, but there are two books that follow this line, written before the war began.

In 1924 an Austrian film company made The City Without Jews based on a book written two years earlier by Hugo Bettauer. At that time, the Nazi Party in Germany was new, tiny and on the lunatic fringe of politics. It barely existed at all in Austria. A year later, Arthur Landsberger's Berlin without Jews took up the theme. The plot line follows the fortunes of two families, the Jewish Oppenheims and the Lutheran Rudenbergs. A far right political party takes control of Germany and deports its Jews as the rest of the country looks on and does nothing.

What is weird about both these books – and films – is that they were eerily prophetic at a time when such a genre barely existed in fiction. But the endings in both are happier than in reality. In Berlin Without Jews, the country realizes that is a poorer place without them and invites them back. In City Without Jews, the whole thing turns out to be a bad dream!

The ghettoes and the death camps were not a bad dream, whatever Holocaust deniers claim today, but both books' authors faced nightmares of their own. Two months after Hitler became Chancellor of Germany, Arthur

Landsberger killed himself. And Hugo Bettauer was murdered soon after the movie premiered, by Otto Rothstock, a hero of the Right who had recently been released from a psychiatric institution.

THE MEN WHO BROKE INTO AUSCHWITZ

!!

When war broke out in September 1939, very few people had ever heard of Oswiecium, an obscure little village in Poland. By 1945, as Auschwitz-Birkenau, it was the most notorious of the death camps and remains today a grim testimony to the Holocaust and the evils of Nazi Germany. To anyone who knows it, it was hell on earth and the last place where anyone would go voluntarily. Or was it?

Witold Pilecki

When Poland fell in the September war, 1939, Witold Pilecki joined the resistance. As veteran of the Polish-Soviet war of

1919-21, he was used to danger and hardship and did not take invasion lying down. Rumours began to spread early in 1940 of a camp being built on the site of an old army barracks which had been converted into a tobacco factory. It was surrounded by stagnant ponds, but the new buildings seemed to include bath-houses and corpse-cellars.

Hitler's plan was to obliterate Poland as a country and the Poles as a race and the Resistance watched every move by the army of occupation. The Wehrmacht had been followed quickly by the SS einsatzgruppen, death squads who rounded up Jews and troublemakers and hanged them from lamp-posts in towns across the country. They routinely rounded up 'undesirables' and herded them into the nearest camp. One of these men, who had loitered deliberately in order to be included, was Pilecki, using the name Tomasz Serafinski. 'Reality and logic,' he wrote, 'disappeared as soon as you went beyond the wires.' As a partisan, he kept his head down while secretly smuggling in food, medication and clothing. He also amassed astonishing information as to how Auschwitz was run.

Pilecki's first reports reached Britain early in 1941, but it was not until later that year that he wrote of a massive extension to the camp called Birkenau. Prisoners died at a frightening rate, overworked and starved in what was regarded as a particularly brutal labour camp. The capos, who carried out routine torture on the prisoners, were often Poles themselves and were worse, if anything, than the German guards.

Anyone who opposed the Nazi regime ended up at Auschwitz. Dissidents, like Pilecki himself, starved and stood for hours in the freezing weather of the parade ground, alongside Jews, homosexuals and gypsies – anyone who did not fit the image of the Aryan elite. Pilecki saw with his own eyes the murder of Maximilian Kolbe, a priest who offered himself in the place of fellow-Pole Francis Gajowniczek, on the grounds that the priest had no family and Gajowniczek was a married man.

While Auschwitz-Birkenau was morphing into a death-camp with genocide being carried out on an industrial scale, nothing was done in the West, despite Pilecki's reports. The decision must have been an agonizing one. Had the British and French been able to bomb the place (and France had fallen by this time) then the SS would have ensured that *everyone* died at Auschwitz. The destruction of railway lines would barely have slowed things down.

Pilecki stayed in the camp until 1943, until he was moved two miles away to work in the bakery. He cut telephone lines, disabled alarms, overpowered a guard and escaped using a cut key. He re-joined the Resistance and wrote *Witold's Report*, a harrowing account still available today.

But fate had not quite finished with Witold Pilecki. He offered his services to the Resistance in Warsaw that had been fighting a grim guerrilla war from the city's sewers for three years. Rumours abounded that Stalin's Red Army was on its way west and, motivated by this, the Poles launched an offensive in April 1943. The SS had vowed to liquidate the ghetto in three days; in fact, it took them twenty-eight. Among the prisoners, fewer than a hundred of them, was Pilecki, who was now interned at another infamous death camp, Treblinka. The camp was liberated by the Americans in April 1945 and Pilecki joined the Polish army as an intelligence officer.

Poland had been a political football for years and with the rise of the 'iron curtain', the country had simply swapped one jack-booted enemy for another. Stalin, although it took the West far too long to realize it, was as much as a murderous psychopath as Hitler. In 1947, Pilecki was caught spying on the Russians, working, in the left-wing propaganda of the time, for 'foreign imperialists'. He was tortured, made the victim of one of Stalin's show trials and executed in 1948. His burial place remains unknown.

Until 1989 when the Berlin Wall fell and everybody could see through the lies and hypocrisy of the communists, Pilecki was forgotten or regarded as a traitor. His reputation has now been fully restored, but no one can quite understand how a man, who could easily have avoided Auschwitz, went there of his own accord.

Denis Avey

Even more bizarre is the story of Denis Avey. Pilecki was a local man, on the spot in terms of Auschwitz, but Avey, as a British army officer, was not. In April 2011, his best-selling book *The Man Who Broke Into Auschwitz* caused a sensation, but there were doubts about the whole thing and the doubts have not gone away.

Avey was taken prisoner and sent to a sub-camp for British POWs called E715. He deliberately swapped places with an inmate of the main camp to find out what went on there. The details that he gave ring true, but those details have been available in the public domain now for years and anyone can access them. Yad Vashem, the World Holocaust Remembrance Centre, have been unable to give Avey the accolade as 'righteous among the nations', granted to outstanding people who helped the Jews during the Holocaust, because they have been unable to find anyone who can effectively corroborate his story.

Another British prisoner of E715, Brian Bishop, said, 'I can't understand how he did it. To do something like that you need to have several people helping on both sides – our side and the Jewish side.' Another POW, Ron Jones, found it hard to believe that a large, well-fed Englishman could blend in unnoticed with starving inmates. Sam Pivnik, sent to Auschwitz from a local ghetto in August 1943 as a 16-year-old, said, 'Avey's story seems to me highly unlikely. Swapping places with an Auschwitz prisoner isn't just risking his own life, but those of everyone else in his block and he was taking a huge risk that he wouldn't be informed on. It isn't a chance that I would have taken. Prisoners in Auschwitz were so desperate you could not take the risk of trusting them.'

The key to it all was probably a Jewish prisoner called Ernst Lobethal whom Avey befriended at E715. The BBC tracked the man down in the United States long after the war but how much he knew of the details of Avey and his venture into the main camp is not clear.

The same problem that we faced for Pilecki goes doubly for Avey. What would prompt a man to go deliberately from the frying pan into the fire and, in Avey's case, why did he take so long to tell the world about it?

MESCHUGGISMUS (THE CULT OF INSANITY)

!!!

In Nazi Germany, because the Führer saw himself as an art guru (he painted very average landscapes and sold them as post cards), anything new and avant garde was denounced as degenerate art. Anyone who liked modern styles – expressionists, impressionists, surrealists, etc. – were lumped into what the Nazi speechmakers called meschuggismus, the cult of insanity.

In fact, the whole Nazi regime was an example of an insane cult. Below are some examples.

Adolf Legalite (Adolf the legal one)
After the failed putsch of the beer-hall in Munich in 1923, Hitler claimed that everything he did afterwards would be within the bounds of the law and he repeated the claim constantly. In fact, if we listed the *illegal* actions carried out by the Fuhrer, it would fill this book.

Ahnenpass (Ancestry passport)
Because the Nazis were obsessed with race, cards were issued to every German which proved their Aryan ancestry. Like all official documents however, these could be faked and big money could be made out of falsifying such cards.

Angstbrosche (brooch of fear)
Members of the Nazi party wore circular, enamel, lapel

badges with the swastika in the centre. Their opponents, a brave and dwindling bunch as time went on, called it the brooch of fear.

Anti-Semit

Long before it was decided that smoking was dangerous, a popular brand of roll-your-own cigarettes in 1920s Germany, was smoked by Nazis. It was called, appropriately, Anti-Semit in line with their opposition to Jews.

Beefsteak Nazis

The original twenty five points of the Nazi Party contained far left ideas. After all, the official name of the group was The National Socialist Workers Party. Although all this was played down later, the concept never went away entirely. 'Beefsteak Nazis' were those whose allegiances were doubtful – brown (the colour of the SA's shirts) on the outside, but red (the Communist colour) on the inside.

'Call me Meier!'

Hermann Goering was absolutely confident that his Luftwaffe (air force) was so superior that no bombs would ever fall on Germany. On 9 August 1939, less than a month before war began, he said 'Not a single bomb will fall on the Ruhr [Germany's Industrial heartland]. If an enemy plane reaches the Ruhr, my name is not Hermann Goering. You can call me Meier!'

Meier was a typical Jewish surname. In the years ahead, how the Reichmarschal must have regretted this boast!

Deutsche Blick (the German glance)

After 1933, it became the custom for Nazis – and eventually all Germans – to greet each other with the straight arm salute and the words, 'Heil Hitler'. In reality, many people avoided this as being too ludicrous. They swivelled their heads from side to side to make sure no-one was looking (the German glance) then greeted each other normally.

<u>Feindhörer (listens to enemy broadcasts)</u>
A key weapon of the Second World War was the radio. It kept morale high and was used by Allies and Axis powers to spread information or disinformation, depending on the situation. Large numbers of Britons, for example, listened to the broadcasts of William Joyce, Lord Haw-Haw, claiming that Britain was finished as a world power. Likewise, agents like Sefton Delmer, who spoke fluent German, let the Nazis know that their regime was doomed. In Nazi-controlled areas, those who listened to such broadcasts, as opposed to Josef Goebbell's official radio outlets, were regarded as enemies of the people. Children were encouraged to shop their offending parents to the authorities.

<u>Góldfasan (the golden pheasants)</u>
The Nazis liked dressing up. Only Mussolini's fascists looked sillier than men like Herman Goering, in his white uniform loaded with medals and gold braid (the sort of thing the British called 'scrambled egg'). The pheasant was used as a stupid, gaudy bird in contrast to the all-powerful eagle which was a German totem, itself pinched from the Romans.

<u>'Heil Hitler!'</u>
The phrase became a legal requirement in Nazi Germany. Every adult was expected to use it as a greeting, extolling the Nazi cult of leadership to a ridiculous level. For children, every school day began with the words and they were expected to use it up to 150 times a day as part of the indoctrination programme.

<u>Honorary Aryans</u>
The problem with a regime that is based on racism is that alliance with other races is difficult. In two glaring examples, however, Hitler ignored the racial inconvenience and got on with it. In 1939 he signed an agreement with Josef Stalin, the Russian leader, to the effect that Germany and the Soviet Union would carve up Poland between them. The famous

cartoon by the British cartoonist David Low, shows Hitler and Stalin greeting each over the corpse of Poland. The Fuhrer is saying 'The scum of the earth, I believe.' Eastern Europeans were the Slavs, a people way down the social scale in Nazi philosophy; likewise, the Japanese. Long before the attack on Pearl Harbor, which effectively made Hitler and Emperor Hirohito allies, a German-Japanese agreement had been signed in November 1936. The common enemy of both countries were the Communists and on that basis the Japanese were made honorary Aryans as a token of Nazi esteem. The term was, of course, a token of Nazi hypocrisy.

Kampfbund Des Gewerblichen Mittelstandes (Militant Association of Retailers).

We still complain about supermarkets and chain stores squeezing out the high street retailes today, but in Nazi Germany, this took on a more sinister term. It is believed that such stores were run by Jews and therefore should be closed down. Many of them were.

'Kinder, Kirche, Küche' (children, church, kitchen)

Women were nowhere in Nazi ideology. Hitler planned, among many other architectural ideas, to build a vast shrine to Nazism in Berlin, with the names of thousands of prominent Nazis chiselled on the marble; not one woman was mentioned. Instead, women's place was in the home and the phrase 'kinder, kirche, kuche' summed it all up. Female emancipation was a product of degenerate thinking, and the various female organisations in Germany, like the League of German Maidens, were merely pale copies of the male originals. Women were engaged to marry Aryans to breed Aryan children. They even received gold, silver and bronze decorations for doing so. Leni Riefenstahl, the director who made the Nazi PR film, *Triumph of the Will,* was almost unique as a woman carrying out the roles of a man.

Lebensborn (The Fountain of Life)

Heinrich Himmler's drive to create an Aryan master-race

that would dominate world affairs for a thousand years led to the Lebensborn programme whereby perfect Aryan specimens, with fair hair and blue eyes, would be made pregnant by SS superstuds. Marriage was not necessary and romantic relationships unimportant. Once pregnant, girls were sent to a special maternity centre where every care was taken of them and their infants. In addition, Aryan children from outside Germany were kidnapped to add to the breeding stock, indoctrinated as good Nazis and adopted by 'racially trustworthy' parents. Thousands of children became victims.

<u>Marzgefallene (those who joined in March)</u>
When Hitler came to power in March 1933 there was a stampede to join the Nazi party. Diehard Nazis who had been there since the early '20s regarded such people with contempt.

<u>Max Heiliger Deposit Account</u>
The mass deportation of Jews and other people decmed undesirable by the Third Reich, meant that, apart from the appalling treatment and loss of life, a vast fortune of belongings of all kind was looted from emptied ghettoes or which ended up on the railway platforms of camps like Auschwitz. The valuables here, including gold fillings from people who had 'gone to the chimneys' were collected in an SS bank account, with the full connivance of the Reichsbank president, Walter Funk, under the fictitious name of the Max Heiliger Deposit. Although some of this treasure was returned after the war, much of it was never recovered, its original owners long since dead.

<u>Pour Le Semit (To the Semite)</u>
The most distinguished military decoration for Germans in the First World War was the Maltese Cross with the French label Pour Le Merite, known as the Blue Max. Pour le Semite was the ironic term used by Nazis for the yellow star of David that Jews were forced to wear in public.

Schleiferi (grinding)

From time to time in the British and American press today, there are shocking stories of horseplay among students and cadets that has got out of hand. The Americans call this 'hazing' and it has a centuries old pedigree. In Nazi Germany, the Hitler Jugend (Hitler Youth) went through this ritual as a matter of routine. The purpose was to make Aryan soldiers out of them and harsh physical punishment was de rigeur. Many boys broke down under this cruel regime, but most put up with it, believing in the justification behind it.

Sitzkreig (The Sitting War)

Britain called it the 'phoney war'. France knew it as 'drôle de guerre' (the funny war), but in Germany the period from September 1939 to May 1940 was the 'sitting war' or 'armchair war'. This is understandable for the British and French because in that time period there was no military activity in the west. In the east, however, on Germany's doorstep, the Wehrmacht was busy invading Poland. Nobody was sitting down through that.

Totenbergen (Castles of the Dead)

Among the vast architectural schemes that Hitler planned for what he believed would be a successful European war, the castles of the dead would have been astounding. They would have been huge variations of the cenotaph in London's Whitehall, one on the Atlantic coast facing west as a token of Germany's achievement in liberating Europe from British influence and the other on the Eastern front where 'the chaotic forces of the East' (Russian) had been overwhelmed. Neither castle got beyond the blueprint stage.

THE MOUSE THAT INVADED

!!!

We have all seen the photographs – the grainy black and white memorials to the men who were part of D-Day, the culmination of Operation Overlord when the Allies set foot on European soil for the first time in three years. The terrifying guns of USS Nevada blasting out against Utah Beach on the coast of Normandy. The scenes in the 'ducks', the amphibian vehicles grinding through the shallows towards 'bloody' Omaha, where 200 Americans would die in minutes. The British commandos, in their khaki and their red berets wading ashore on Sword Beach, keeping their rifles above the water line.

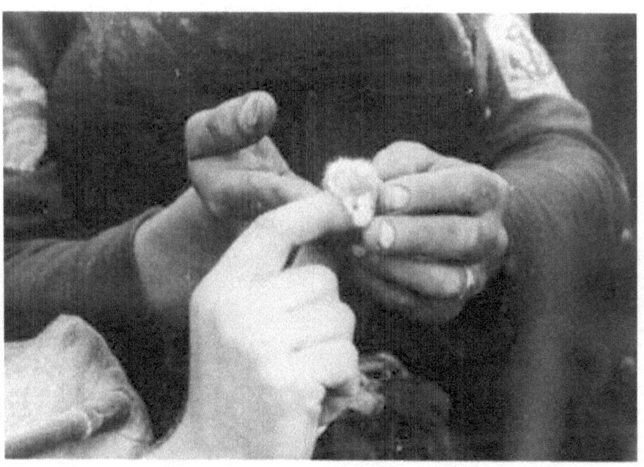

To those of us of a younger generation, we have all seen *The Longest Day* and *Saving Private Ryan*, two incomparable war movies that have recaptured that dazzling and horrific episode in history.

What we probably have not seen is the photograph of one of the most unlikely 'combatants' with the Allied Invasion. 156,000 soldiers hit those beaches on 6 June 1944, the day of deliverance, and in somebody's pocket, on one of the landing crafts, was Eustace, a piebald mouse who was a regimental pet. It is not known what deeds of valour he witnessed or exactly what part he played, but we know, from the photograph, that he was there. And we know he survived to get back home again.

THE MYTHS AND MIRACLES OF DUNKIRK

!

When is a victory not a victory? When it is left in the hands of Winston Churchill's government and a compliant media at a desperate time in British history.

In simple terms, the British Expeditionary Force, commanded by Lord Gort, was driven back to the French coast, wrong-footed by the speed of the German advance under Gerd von Rundstedt. They ended up on the coast of Normandy around the previously anonymous little town of Dunkerque. This was in May 1940. Churchill had recently taken over from Neville Chamberlain as prime minister and *somehow* the thousands of men on the French beaches had to be rescued. Enter myth, propaganda and situations that still, eighty years on, have yet to be explained.

In nine days between 26 May and 3 June, almost 338,000 Allied troops, including Frenchmen, were evacuated, giving rise to the Dunkirk spirit, fortress Britain and even a victory against impossible odds. The BBC claimed that the BEF had 'come back to glory'. The *Daily Telegraph*'s banner headline read 'Defeat Turned to Victory'. Let us look at the reality.

The Thin Red Line

One of the myths of Dunkirk is that the BEF was outnumbered. It wasn't. The Allies had a million more men than the Axis powers and five extra divisions.

<u>Gas! Gas!</u>
The rumour spread that the Germans were using gas, like the phosphorus of the First World War, in defiance of the Geneva Convention. They weren't.

The real situation was that the British Army was not ready, in terms of weapons, equipment and training. As Field Marshal Bernard Montgomery wrote after the war, 'In September 1939, the British Army was totally unfit to fight a first class war on the continent of Europe' – and little had changed by May 1940.

<u>The Impossibility of a German Victory</u>
British troops believed wholeheartedly in the smug, over-positive view of the media, which extolled their preparedness, guts and knowhow. The lightning advance of von Rundstedt's panzers exposed the inadequacy of the French and British armies. France fell in six weeks, largely due to its own incompetence.

<u>The British Soldier is Second to None</u>
There are many examples of this being true, but in the spring of 1940, the second line troops were badly trained and led. Not one of the Territorial brigades withstood the German assault. The retreating mob seen by Lt Hadley, an infantry officer, says it all – 'a disorderly mob of soldiers, grimy, bloodstained and badly scared … very much like the popular conception of the Italian army'.

26 May was declared a national day of prayed and the Archbishop of Canterbury spoke over the wireless to bewildered households all over the country. Everyone hoped for a miracle. In fact, the first of the Dunkirk miracles had already happened. Two days earlier, Hitler halted the German advance, for reasons still debated by military historians. Were the Wehrmacht exhausted, needing time to regroup? Did Hitler want to appease the British in order to

secure a peace-deal? Or was he, as many contended at the time, simply mad?

The weather turned against the Germans too. Poor visibility made Luftwaffe attacks on Dunkirk impossible – although, of course, the same was true of the RAF, who were accused of abandoning the army. It was even claimed that smoke from German artillery drifted westwards and covered the men being evacuated from the beaches.

The 850 'little ships', many owned and piloted by civilians along the south coast, provided a hitherto unprecedented armada to get desperate men off the sands. It was an extraordinary event, but these boats only got 26,000 (8 per cent of the total) out of France; the rest was down to the Royal Navy. The boats did indeed provide ammunition and vital supplies and the heroism of those civilians should not be underestimated. Whether this constitutes a 'miracle' is another question.

Lastly, there was the millpond surface of the English Channel, famous for its usual choppiness, which allowed both the little ships and the navy to operate effectively.

The loss of equipment was a major blow and

recriminations followed for years that the RAF had not done their bit and, from the French, that Britain had abandoned is ally. In fact, 47,000 French troops were evacuated, ready to fight another day.

Dunkirk was a defeat, pure and simple. But would it have been even worse without the 'miracles' in the paragraphs above?

THE NIGHT WITCHES

!!

Walpurgisnacht is celebrated in Germany on the eve of St Walpurga's day, 1 May. It is the equivalent of the British and American Halloween, a time when the witches ride, swarming through the air on horse and broomstick, accompanied by shrieking devils. They head for the mountains like the Brocken or the Blockburg, dancing like maniacs in an orgy with the devil.

But the *Nachthexen* (night witches) of the Second World War were not the lurid imaginings of Renaissance Europe or occult writers from Aleister Crowley to Stephen King. They were real. They were Russian. And they were deadly.

I have in front of me a photograph of these women, relaxing at a forward airbase somewhere on the Eastern Front in 1944. Some are making tea, probably to be drunk the Russian way, sucking it through a sugar cube. They are all in their twenties, in the shapeless Cossack-style uniforms worn by their men. They are smoking and chatting, comfortable in their fur-lined flying boots. Only one of them has seen the camera and she is checking her hair and smiling.

Traditionally, women had no place in war. They waved a tearful goodbye to their menfolk all over the world before 1914-18, urging those men to do their bit for king and country and even giving them the white feather of cowardice if they did not sign up. All that changed during the First World War, with women taking over male roles on the land and in the factories. A handful had been nurses long before Florence Nightingale made the job respectable in the Crimea

(1854-6) but now those numbers swelled. War became up-close and personal in 1914-18 and remained so between 1939 and '45. The Second World War in particular was the 'people's war' and the Home Front was as real and dangerous a place as distant battlefields used to be.

The Russian experience was different. Even before the Revolution of 1917, women were allowed to raise their own fighting battalions. Determined feminists like Elena Tsebrzhinskaya, dressed as men to be allowed to serve as nurses at the Front. In the Revolution itself, shaven-headed 'death battalions' fought both for and against the Bolsheviks, trying to create order in a broken, chaotic society or establish a brave new world, depending on whose side they were on.

Russia was no more ready for the Second World War than Britain or France. The hopeful dreams of 1917 had morphed into the nightmare of Josef Stalin, the Union of Soviet Socialist Republics and blind obedience to the state. First happy to ally with Hitler to partition Poland and add to his already vast empire, the 'Red Tsar', Stalin', had to switch allegiance abruptly in June 1941 when the Third Reich launched Operation Barbarossa and invaded the Soviet Union. Russia had been a backward power for two hundred years; modernity and technology had passed her by and the intransigent, blinkered Communist state did little to remedy that. The Russian strategy in wartime, apart from allowing the appalling winter weather – 'generals Janvier and Fevrier' – to wipe out invasions, was throw thousands of men to their deaths. Stalin was doing this with a vengeance after 1941.

Among his cannon fodder was a group that turned out to be rather elite – the all-female 588th Night Bomber regiment. But if the unit was elite, the aircraft were not. The Polikarpov Po-2 was an outdated biplane, literally made of plywood and they were no match for the state-of-the-art Messerschmitts of the Luftwaffe. There were no cockpits and the fuselage was so cold in the Russian winter that touching them would rip skin from fingers. They had no radios and their slow speed meant that as daytime fighters, they were useless.

After dark, however, it was a different story. The Po-2 was too small to be picked up on enemy radar and, like the flimsy aircraft of the First World War could land and take off virtually anywhere. They carried two bombs at a time (their maximum weight load) and each plane made eight to eighteen sorties a night. Over their targets, the pilots switched off their engines and let the aircraft glide, with a swishing sound like a witch's broom.

So successful was the 588th that the Germans gave them the name Nachthexen, believing that they were desperate homicidal criminals sent on forlorn-hope missions. They were also rumoured to have been injected with a new chemical to enable them to see in the dark. The unit became the most decorated female outfit of the war but were not allowed to take part in Stalin's lavish victory parade and were disbanded six months later. For them, the patriotic war was over.

AN OFFICER AND A GENTLEMAN

!!!

If your name is Digby Tatham-Warter, what else could you become but an army officer? Digby was born in 1917 and his father was in the trenches of the Western Front that year; he died as a result of gas poisoning when Digby was eleven. At the age of twenty, Digby graduated from the Royal Military College at Sandhurst and, as a commissioned officer, was sent out to India.

The brightest jewel in the Imperial Crown was fading by then and the ever-growing number of those clamouring for India's independence, wanted the British out. Even so, true to the long history of British rule in the sub-continent, Tatham-Warter enjoyed tiger-hunting, and pig-sticking, both of which would fill today's 'woke brigade' with horror. He thought nothing of 'borrowing' an American Dakota bomber and flying the officers of his company to London's Ritz hotel for a party.

It is highly likely that Tatham-Warter was a throw back. He never got on with radio signals as a means of communication and relied on bugle calls instead, once essential on the battlefields of Europe. Passwords were not for him either, especially as the high command were constantly changing them, so he took to carrying an umbrella with him all the time, if only to prove to Allied support troops that he was an Englishman!

Arnhem has gone down in military history as a 'bridge

too far' when, in September 1944, the Allies were brought to an abrupt halt by unexpectedly fierce German resistance in the Low Countries. Parachuted into Holland on the night of the 17th, Digby snuck his men, commando-style, through back gardens rather than main roads, taking 150 prisoners en route. They reached the bridge at Arnhem at 8pm and ran into enemy fire. True to form, their radio packed up and Tatham-Warter put his bugler to good use. The German counter-attack, which included panzers, did not faze the commander at all. Wearing an actual bowler hat, as opposed to the 'battle bowler', he led a bayonet charge, waving his umbrella at astonished soldiers of the Wehrmacht, who had never seen anything like it. One soldier probably never saw much again as Tatham-Warter jabbed his umbrella through the eye-slit of an armoured car and took the driver's eye out!

The umbrella was doubly useful that day. Tatham-Warter's chaplain was pinned down by enemy fire trying to reach the wounded. The commander opened the umbrella, which of course was no defence against bullets at all, and got the man to safety. Lieutenant Pat Barnett, who witnessed all this, asked him why the !*!* he carried the umbrella. 'Oh my goodness, Pat,' Tatham-Warter said, 'what if it rains?'

The fight was hopelessly one-sided and eventually Tatham-Warter and Barnett were captured. The last bugle call sounded, blasting out *God Save the King*.

For a man who had fought at Arnhem, a German field hospital was not a problem. He and Barnett escaped and made it to Dutch civilians who disguised them as a painter and decorator. Digby Tatham-Warter became Peter Jensen, the deaf-mute son of a lawyer, in that speaking Walloon was not one of the officer's accomplishments. So cunning was the disguise that even when German soldiers were billeted with the Jensens, they never suspected a thing. In the end, together with 150 other escapees, Tatham-Warter cycled his way across Holland to take part in Operation Pegasus.

Had the battle of Arnhem been the success the Allies hoped for, the war might have been shortened by six months. No blame can be attached to the men who fought there. And as for Digby Tatham-Warter, they just do not make men like him any more!

THE ONE-EYED GHOST

!

Of all the countries of the British empire to do their bit for King and Country, Canada was a front runner. 'Nobody' a Wehrmacht general said ruefully in 1942 'fights like the Canadians'. And the war-time career of one Canadian, Leo Major, is proof-positive of this.

He enlisted in Le Régiment de la Chaudière, based in Quebec in 1940 and took part in Operation Overlord, landing on the Normandy beaches on 6 June 1944. In a gun-fight with four German soldiers, and a half-track, he was partially blinded in his left eye by a phosphorous grenade. He made the point that sniper like him only needed one good eye and he fought the rest of the war with an iconic eye patch over the useless one.

In the heavy fighting around the River Scheldt in October, Major captured 93 Germans single-handedly. His plan had been to capture only two, but his rate of fire was such that dozens of the enemy threw down their rifles. In an appalling act of self-destruction, the Waffen-SS, always the most fanatical element of the German army, opened fire on Major's prisoners, killing seven of them. When his Bren Carrier struck a land mine, Major was thrown into the air, breaking both ankles as he fell. As with the eye wound, he refused to be evacuated home and waited at a base hospital while his leg-bones knitted.

Major's finest moment, and one still shrouded in mystery, was the action at Zwolle in the Netherlands, in April 1945. The Medieval town was heavily fortified and Major and Corporal Wilfrid Arsenault volunteered to undertake a reconnaissance mission. They were caught and Arsenault was killed. Major went on a one-man mission to take Zwolle. Carrying two Sten guns and a handful of grenades, he made as much noise as possible in the early hours. The garrison were largely asleep and the sentries were not ready for what they assumed was a large liberation force. They ran and Zwolle was indeed liberated.

While all this sounds like a Boys' Own adventure, it is difficult to explain Zwolle's fall any other way. Major got lucky, that was certain, but he also had extraordinary courage. 'The one-eyed ghost' went on to fight with his accustomed bravery in the Korean War too and became the only Canadian to receive a DCM in two different conflicts.

OPERATION MISTLETOE

!!!

In the black art of espionage, all rules of conventional warfare were off. Knowing your enemy was key to success in any military operation and it was known, or at least generally believed, that many leading Nazis were obsessed with astrology and omens. There is a very long history of all this from the British point of view; John Dee, Elizabeth I's magus, not only advised the monarch about the right and wrong time to make vital decisions, he also worked with Francis Walsingham, the queen's spymaster, to undermine Catholics and *the* threat to Britain in the sixteenth century, Philip II's Spain.

In fact, it was German Intelligence who began the use of astrology in the Second World War. Before America's entry to the war in December 1941, German agents operated freely in the United States, prophesying Reich victories and the collapse of the Reich's enemies. Given the whirlwind success of blitzkrieg in the war's opening months, this was neither difficult nor supernatural, but gullible people bought it all nonetheless.

British Intelligence, the SIS, countered this by focussing on the natural interest in the occult which they believed was paramount in the minds of Hitler, his deputy Rudolf Hess, Heinrich Himmler, head of the SS, Alfred Rosenberg, the Nazi ideologist and an arguable 2,000 others! Cecil Williamson took all this a stage further. Calling himself a neopagan warlock, he founded the Witchcraft Research Centre and a museum of witchcraft which has moved around

Britain in the years since its creation. Now at Boscastle in Cornwall, it had earlier existed at Bourton-on-the-Water in the Cotswolds.

Williamson's idea was to set up a centre for astrological espionage at Ashdown Forest in Sussex, one of the 'haunted' places of Britain associated with pre-Christian ritual and ceremony. Forty Canadian soldiers, with a radio transmitter code-named Aspidistra, took part in elaborate rituals to predict the future for the Third Reich. This was Operation Mistletoe.

The whole thing could be shelved under the heading of 'nonsense', the sixty per cent of espionage undertakings that the Macmillan theory says do not work. *Except* that a night chosen of great astrological significance was 10 May 1941, when six planets were aligned in Taurus and conjoined to a full moon. That was the night of the worst London blitz of the entire war. It was also the night when a lone Be 110 was spotted flying over Scotland. Its pilot bailed out and the plane crashed. He gave his name to the arresting authorities as Hauptmann Alfred Horn. In fact, he was Rudolf Hess, Hitler's *stellvertreter* (deputy), nominally the second most important man in the Third Reich, and a great believer in horoscopes. Had a secret agent reported the Ashdown Forest shenanigans to him and had he timed his flight to coincide with the planets' movements?

What is indisputable is that as soon as Hess's flight became public knowledge, Hitler launched the Aktion Hess, a rounding up of hundreds of German fortune-tellers, astrologers and cranks. Perhaps the Fuhrer realised that the stars were never on his side, after all.

THE PIGEON MYSTERY

!!

Anyone today who has open fires is familiar with the problem. Unless the cowling on chimney tops is secure, birds of every feather will fly downwards, looking for…whatever birds look for. David Martin had this problem at his home in Bletchingley, Surrey, in 2012 when he cleared out his chimney. The bones of a pigeon came down with the soot and he thought little of it until he noticed a small red capsule attached to a leg bone. He was able to unscrew it and found inside a coded message on paper.

The message was written by Sergeant W. Stott, to a recipient known only as 'XO2'. Intrigued, Martin sent copies of the message to GCHQ, the high security in Cheltenham and to the museum at Bletchley Park, the famous code-breaking centre that unravelled the Enigma mystery.

Coded messages had long been used by soldiers and agents in war and peace time, around the world, but there were problems in deciphering this one. The cracking of codes depended on two parties, the sender and receiver, having the same explanatory code-books. These were changed regularly to prevent vital information (like Enigma) falling into enemy hands. As GCHQ admitted, without the original code books they were stymied. Despite the assertion by some people that they have cracked the code, we are no further forward. There is speculation that the message was sent either to Bomber Command or to Field Marshal Montgomery's headquarters at Reigate, not far from David Martin's home.

The pigeon took its secret to a smoky grave.

THE RED BOOK

!!

The gung-ho war movies of the 1950s portray a stoic British nation, usually embodied by lantern-jawed actors like Jack Hawkins and Anthony Steele, united in a patriotic cause against the tyranny of Nazi Germany. Actually, it was not quite like that. As in *The Gauleiter of the Bahamas*, there were elements of the aristocracy in particular who were not only pro-peace (the Hitler appeasers like Neville Chamberlain) but anti-Bolshevik, anti-Semitic and pro-Nazi.

Nowhere was this more obvious than in the creation of the Right Club in 1939, shortly before the outbreak of war. Their names – 135 men and 100 women – were listed in a lockable, leather-bound ledger called the Red Book. Had the Germans successfully invaded in the summer of 1940, which was the plan, these 'fellow travellers of the Right' would have been heroes.

The leader of the club was Archibald Maude Ramsay, an MP and minor Scots aristocrat who left the group because Oswald Mosley, also an MP, effectively took it over. Together with the Link, another pro-German group, there were several thousand people in pre and early war Britain who were rightly regarded with suspicion by MI5 and Churchill's government. Some of them left the groups when war was declared, but others stayed on, making broadcasts on behalf of the 'New British Broadcasting Service' from Germany that was busy counting 'the lies' of the Jewish-owned BBC proper!

Ramsay gave the Red Book to the American embassy

in London. The United States did not join the war until December 1941 and Ramsay no doubt hoped that the list, effectively on American neutral soil, would be safe from the British authorities. The Scotsman had sensitive documents from Churchill to Chamberlain at this crucial – and confused – time in British politics, and he believed that publication of these papers would dissuade the States, under President F.D. Roosevelt from joining the war.

In the event, MI5 moved faster. The Red Book fell into their hands and lots of the list were arrested as would-be enemy agents under the new Defence Regulation 18B. Ramsey himself, Oswald Mosley and his wife, Diane Mitford and Sir Barry Domville, once director of naval intelligence, all found themselves behind bars.

SANTA'S WARS

!!

In the irreligious twenty-first century, the most persistent surviving myth relating to St Nicholas (Santa Claus) is that he lives in Lapland, working hard all year round with his faithful team of elves to make the toys he then delivers to all good children at Christmas time.

The Lapps, who call themselves Samelat, can be found across the modern state frontiers of Norway, Sweden, Finland and Russia, with a sizeable colony in Alaska. They are a shamanic people, like the Inuit, worshipping the bear, not a white-bearded old man driving reindeer, although the Scandinavian Lapps are reindeer-nomads. With the coming of Christianity, most of them became Lutheran.

The Second World War, for most of us in the West, is seen as a continuous struggle from 1939 to '45 but in Finland, it forms three distinct campaigns. The first was the Winter War (30 November 1939-13 March 1940) when, in accordance with the Ribbentrop-Molotov agreement, the Soviet Union invaded. Britain and France were sympathetic to the Lapps. Although the Russo-German accord was secret, no free people were happy with unjustified invasion. The problem was that the west had its hands full against the speed and power of the German blitzkrieg and could not help the Finns out. In fact, the Finnish army, used to their vicious winters and equipped for them, fought the Russians to a standstill. Stalin, of course, had a dozen excuses: the winder was worse than usual (it wasn't); the Mannerheim Line was stronger than the Maginot (it wasn't); and the Americans had sent a thousand pilots to bolster up the fledgling Finnish air force (they hadn't).

The second campaign was the Continuation War (25 June 1941-19 September 1944). With no help from the west (despite America's involvement by this time) the Finns chose the lesser of two evils and joined the Axis to regain the territory taken from them by the Russians. Somehow, the fighting spirit of the Winter War had gone. The Finns got no further than Leningrad and stayed there for years.

The third campaign was the Lapland War (15 September 1944-27 April 1945). The Soviet Union gave Finland an ultimatum – kick the Germans out of their territories or face the consequences. This was a grim task, as the Wehrmacht retreated westward carrying out a scorched earth policy and leaving nothing but devastation in their wake.

Finland's political position in the Second World War was unique. It changed sides twice and was the only democracy allied with the Axis powers. It was also the only country east of Germany that did not become a Russian puppet behind the Iron Curtain from 1946. And Helsinki, the capital, was the only capital in Europe, other than London and Moscow, that did not fall to the enemy.

One of the Lapland towns that was obliterated in the

German retreat was Rovaniemi. It was rebuilt by architect alvar Aalto in a reindeer-shaped street grid and Eleanor Roosevelt, widow of the American president, made a surprise visit there in 1950 to launch Roosevelt Cottage, a UNICEF project. Originally a Luftwaffe airfield, the local airport was renamed Santa's official Airport and Santa's Village stands over an old Wehrmacht barracks, visited by thousands of tourists every year. Seven hundred thousand letters from children around the world reach Rovaniemi every year.

Let's hope that Father Christmas will never see another war in his homeland!

THE SCHOOLGIRL AND THE SPITFIRE

!!

The Second World War has been called the 'Wizard's War' – never before had so much ingenious technology been used to defeat an enemy.

Captain Fred Hill was a 'boffin', a scientific officer working for the British Air Ministry, itself a novel organization in terms of the history of warfare. His particular area of expertise was the development of Supermarine Spitfires and Hawker Hurricanes, the fighter aircraft that have an iconic status today. Each plane was equipped with four cannon (the obsolete term for guns was still officially in use) and Hill doubted whether that would be enough in aerial duels with the enemy.

In the 1930s, everybody was working in the dark. The threat was from aggressive, ambitious Nazi Germany but the official government line from prime ministers Stanley Baldwin and Neville Chamberlain, was one of appeasement – work with Herr Hitler and all would be well. Behind the scenes, however, more pragmatic minds had to prepare for any eventuality. The Luftwaffe was an unknown force. In theory, the Treaty of Versailles had severely limited the size of Germany's armed forces – the air force could only fly gliders, for example. In practice, Herman Goering's Luftwaffe were building aircraft secretly in Soviet Russian territory – Dorniers, Heinkels and Messerschmitts.

The military dictum was that 'the bomber will always

get through' because bombing was a new and terrifying concept. Only German bombing of Guernica in the Spanish Civil War stood to bear witness to just how terrifying. Captain Hill wanted to balance the odds. Convinced that four guns per fighter would be inadequate, he spent night after night at his kitchen table, working with his 13-year-old daughter, Hazel, to calculate trajectories, rates of fire and gun-weight. Hazel was what today we would call dyslexic, but her grasp of numbers was astonishing and if Dad could not work it out, Hazel could. Hill presented his findings to the Air Ministry, proving that the eight-gun nay-sayers were wrong; eight guns would not slow a fighter plane appreciably and the fire-power advantage was incalculable. The Ministry was impressed – eight guns it was.

The result was the unprecedented Battle of Britain, with dog-fights snarling over the skies of southern England. The Luftwaffe was outfought because it was outgunned – thanks to Captain Hill and his girl. In 2020 the remarkable story was told in a BBC documentary *The Schoolgirl Who Helped To Win a War.*

THE SECOND BOOK

!

Hitler's 'great opus', part autobiography, part mission statement, was *Mein Kampf* (My Struggle) written in Landsberg prison in 1924. After a failed coup in Munich, the Nazi party was broken up and everybody assumed that the world would hear no more about it. For Hitler however, it was only just beginning. With help from the university-educated Rudolff Hess (in gaol with him) and Hess's mentor, Professor Karl Haushofer, her wrote a pseudo-philosophical rant, mostly about the purity of the Aryan race, which became the bible of Nazism. When Hitler came to power in 1933, *Mein Kampf* was a must-have. Every German household was expected to buy one, making the Fuhrer a millionaire in his own right. Lavish leather-bound copies were given to Aryan newly-weds as wedding presents and the book was translated into dozens of languages to be sold world-wide.

But Hitler wrote a sequel. Or did he? The *Zweites Buch* (Second Book) was written supposedly in 1928, by which time the Nazis had re-emerged as a growing political force in Weimar Germany and the terrifying SS had been set up. Put together with *Mein Kampf*, the second book was a diatribe against the Jews, but it is also a blue-print for what would happen if the Nazis assumed power. Germany would ally with Italy, as the Fascist 'fellow travellers' and with Britain, because of the Saxon racial links and the fact that Britain had no political ambition in Europe, content with its vast colonial empire. France was the enemy in the west (as it had been long before 1871 when the German state was first set up) and once she was defeated, Hitler's new Reich would head a crusade against Poland and the Soviet Union.

The second book's take on America is fascinating, and accords with the confusion and lack of clarity of most of Hitler's prognostications. Perhaps because there were so many Jews in the United States and because the country had joined the Allies in the First World War, America was seen as an ongoing threat. On the other hand, the equally powerful German lobby in the White House corridors of power, as well as the country's toxic attitude to blacks and Native Americans made the culture of the United States something to be admired.

The type-written drafts of the *Zweite Buch* was locked in a safe in the offices of Eher Verlag, who had published *Mein Kampf*. In 1928 sales of the first book were dwindling. It was arguably the catastrophic financial chaos of the Wall Street crash the following year that made Nazism topical again. Perhaps this was why the publishers quietly forgot about it. Found, along with much else pertaining to the Hitler years, by the US Army in 1945, it was finally published by Gerhard Weinberg in 1958 and then with notations two years later by Deutsche Verlagsanstalt of Stuttgart. An English edition did not appear until 2003.

The question remains; how much of the second book is actually Hitler? Bearing in mind the input of Hess and Haushofer in *Mein Kampf*, it is likely that there was similar co-operation for the sequel. That said, had the book been published before 1933, it might have made the appeasers of crypto-Nazism in Europe, rather more realistic in their dealings with Hitler.

SLINKY

!

Every post war generation has been enthralled by it, the sight of a tightly coiled metal spring tumbling down flights of stairs and falling from high places. It fascinated toddlers who could watch Slinkies doing their stuff for hours. And it fascinated them all over again at secondary school when their Physics teachers explained the science behind it.

What is not generally known is that Slinky was a child of the Second World War. In 1943, mechanical engineer Richard James was investigating ways to keep sensitive ship equipment safe at sea. He accidentally knocked some samples of a shelf, watching then expanding gracefully rather than falling and breaking. James could also see, after the war, the beauty of a Slinky as a child's toy – he thought of the name as a commercial selling-point but he and his wife Betty were disappointed to find that nobody wanted to know.

All that changed in late 1945 when Gimbels Department Store in London let James run a demonstration on the shop's stairs. Shoppers were fascinated – the stock of 400 sold out in minutes. Two hundred and fifty million Slinkies later, they still have a place in our hearts, appealing to kids big and small.

THE SPEAR OF DESTINY

!

'One of the soldiers,' St John's gospel tells us, 'pierced His side with a lance and immediately there came out blood and water.' The crucifixion of Christ is described in the New Testament but only John has the story of the spear. The blood of the wound symbolized Christ's humanity and the water represented divinity, according to the first church council at Nicea convened by the emperor Constantine in 325AD. It is the rather spurious Gospel of Nicodemus that gives the soldier a name – Longinus – and a later tradition still calls him a centurion, the officer in charge of at least eighty men in a Roman legion.

The lance, which would probably have been a hasta, a thrusting spear as opposed to a thrown javelin, a pilum, became one of many famous religious relics in the Middle Ages. The true cross, the crown of thorns and the lance were venerated throughout Medieval Christendom, but it is noticeable that there were several of them. At least four examples of the lance, or portions of it, existed simultaneously in the fourteenth century. It is the one in Vienna that brings us forward to the Second World War and Adolf Hitler.

The notion that Hitler and more specifically Heinrich Himmler, head of the SS, was involved in the black arts was not generally held during the war, although Lewis Spence's *The Occult Causes of the Present War* (1943) claimed that there was a Satanic element in Nazism. Hitler himself is on record as saying that any attempt to recreate Wotan (the Norse god Odin) was dead in the water because Christianity had such a hold on Europe. Spence was a conspiracy theorist before the term existed, maintaining that Hitler was 'the creature of shadowy people', whatever that meant.

Since the war, a plethora of books has been written which attempt to link the Nazi's Ultima Thule society via Karl Haushofer, the geopolitician, Himmler's SS HQ in the castle of Wewelsburg and his supposed attempts to establish an archaeological basis for the existence of a pure-bred Aryan society in ancient history. One of the best-known books on the lance's symbolic significance is Trevor Ravenscroft's *The Spear of Destiny* (1973) which has all the hallmarks of an Indiana Jones film. Ravenscroft served with the Royal Fusiliers during the war and was captured during a raid on Rommel's HQ in Libya in November 1941. Ravenscroft's source was Walter Stein who claimed to have known Hitler when he was a struggling art student in Vienna before the First World War. The future Fuhrer, claimed Stein, 'attained higher levels of consciousness by means of drugs and made a penetrating study of medieval occultism and ritual magic'.

According to Stein/Ravenscroft, Longinus' spear, which was believed to have been acquired by the Habsburgs before the collapse of the Austro-Hungarian empire in 1918, was grabbed by Hitler after the *Anschluss* (union) with Austria in 1938. It had magical powers and whoever owned it could rule the world.

The movements of the lance in 1945 are obscure. It may have been part of the regalia discovered by historian Walter Horn, working with the Monuments, Fine Arts and Archives Program under General Patton's Third Army. The work of this dedicated little group was celebrated recently by George Clooney's movie *The Monuments Men*.

As for Himmler's links with the occult, a great deal of nonsense has been written over the last forty years. He was a 'planetary doppelganger', an 'anti-human in a human body', rather than a failed chicken farmer with murderous and anti-Semitic tendencies.

The spear itself is currently on display in the Hofburg Museum in Vienna. It was tested metallurgically in 2003 in laboratory conditions and was dated as seventh or eighth century, about the time that Charlemagne (who was once believed to have owned it) was crowned emperor of the West (AD 800). In its shape and design, the weapon bears no relation to anything carried by the Romans.

SUBMARINE TANKS

!!

By the beginning of the Second World War, the tank had come of age. From the hopeful line-drawings of Leonardo da Vinci, to the clumsy inadequate 'ironclads' of Cambrai in the First World War, tanks had made a slow and hesitant start. By 1939 however, the cavalry was born again in motorized vehicles that ran on caterpillar tracks and could cope with almost any rough terrain. Heinz Guderian's panzers crashed through the forest of the Ardennes as part of the blitzkrieg that hit the west in 1940 and Bernard Montgomery's Crusaders halted the advance of the Afrika Korps at El Alamein.

It was a different story with the Panzerkampfwagen III als Tauchpanzer which was an underwater variant designed in 1940 for the planned invasion of Britain, Operation Sea Lion. Once the Royal Air Force had been overwhelmed by the Luftwaffe (so ran the strategic theory of the German High Command), there would be a small window of opportunity for the Kriegsmarine (German navy) to launch assault troops on British soil. What could be more terrifying than tanks roaring up out of the surf and snarling up English beaches on the south coast? Prototypes were built and proved successful.

An estimated 168 Tauchpanzers were built but because of the RAF's success in the Battle of Britain, there was no opportunity to use them in the Channel. Instead, they were used in river crossings in Operation Barbarossa, the invasion of Soviet Russia in June 1941. Most of them were converted to land vehicles later in the war.

THE SWORD OF ISLAM

!

Leptis Magna is one of the largest excavated sites of Roman civilisation in the world. Until recently, a well-informed Libyan archaeologist would show tourists around, marvelling at the architecture and the full-size chariot circus at the sea's edge. When he came to a few lumps of concrete topped by twisted metal, he was less fulsome in his praise. This, he said, was what the Italians had built in 1930, under the dictator Benito Mussolini and it was noticeable that they were in worse condition than the surrounding buildings which were two thousand years older!

Mussolini had delusions of grandeur and wanted to recreate the Roman Empire which had been the most impressive in the ancient world. It included a broad sweep of North Africa from Morocco in the west to Egypt in the east. Accordingly, Italians settled in Libya, bringing with them western culture and Christianity. By the early 30s, a third of the population of Tripoli and Benghazi was Italian. Inevitably, tensions rose and over a ten year period, an estimated 100,000 people were killed in local rebellions and harsh reprisals by Mussolin's 'new Rome'.

Il Duce was not a religious man, but he understood the need to make his African colonies work. He set up mosques and Quaranic schools and referred to Libyans as 'Italian Muslims of the fourth shore of Italy'. By championing Islam, he hoped to impress other Muslims in Algeria, and British Muslims in Egypt. It was not a success.

In 1937 Mussolini visited Libya, entering Tripoli riding

on a white horse like a Roman Emperor, at the head of 2,600 cavalrymen. A huge statue of his was erected in the city, only to be hauled down by the Allies in 1943. At that triumphal entry in 1937, the Berber Chief Iusuf Kerisc presented the Italian with a curved scimitar, known as the Sword of Islan, the traditional gift for a successful (and popular) military commander. In fact, Mussolini was neither of these things and the sword was just as fake. It was not Berber, nor Libyan nor even Islamic. It was made to Mussolini's specification by an Italian art firm!

The sword was displayed in the summer residence of the dictator, Rocca delle Caminate, an iconic totem of Mussolini as some kind of descendent of the Ottoman Turks and the 'protector of Islam'. It did not make sense and did not fool anybody. When the Caminate estate was overrun by Italian partisans who had turned against their leader in 1943, the sword disappeared and has never been seen since.

UNCLE ADOLF

!

Hitler, they say, loved children and dogs. Several of the children of his closest advisers, such as Josef Goebbels and, in the early days, Putzi Hanfstaengel, called him 'Uncle Adolf' and found him great fun. But one of the many myths about the Fuhrer is that he really did have a nephew, William Patrick Hitler and there is a connection with Liverpool.

The story has been accepted by some historians that between November 1912 and April 1913, Hitler lived with relatives in the city. The tale belongs, in a way, to various countries centuries ago hijacking Jesus Christ. His mother Mary went to live in Gaul (France) after the crucifixion. His disciple, James, sailed to Spain in a stone boat. Jesus himself visited England (then on the edge of the Roman province of Britannia) in the company of his uncle, Joseph of Arimathea. Even by these standards, however, Hitler the Scouser takes some beating!

The tale probably originated in a typescript written in 1940 by Brigid Dowling-Hitler, the wife of Adolf's half brother Alois. The couple's son, William Patrick, according to *My Brother-in-Law Adolf*, was taken to Germany to be brought up as a good Nazi before Brigid, having chatted to such luminaries as Hess and Himmler, got him out. Robert Payne, in *The Life and Death of Adolf Hitler*, accepts the Dowling-Hitler memoir and claims that this explains Hitler's delay at Dunkirk, giving the BEF time to evacuate and his various attempts at peace with Britain.

In fact, Hitler was living in Vienna in 1912-13 and never visited Britain at all.

Nevertheless, stories still survive of William Patrick trying to blackmail the Fuhrer with 'evidence' of his Jewish ancestry within the family. There are other rumours that various off-shoots of the Hitlers have made a pact not to reproduce, so that the bloodline dies out. Contrary to the myth of the blue-eyed children of *The Boys from Brazil*, however, there is no evidence that anti-Semitic megalomania is either genetic or hereditary!

THE UNLIKELY AGENT

!!!

A blind soldier lies in the psychiatric ward of Pasewalk hospital, Bavaria. It is mid-November 1918 and the bloodiest war in history has just finished. Millions are dead and Germany is in ruins. The blind soldier is a decorated hero, with the Iron Cross and the Black Wound Badge to his credit. Captain Karl Mayr, head of the army Information department says of him, 'He would have worked for a Jewish or a French employer just as readily as for an Aryan. When I first met him, he was like a tired stray dog looking for a master.' His name is Adolf Hitler.

We all have an image of the Fuhrer born of the propaganda, pro- and anti- Nazi which grew up in the 1920s and continued to 1945 and beyond. We know the broad events of those years because they are so astonishing and terrifying. It is when we dissect a monster's life that we find evidence that is not just weird, but almost defies belief.

During the First World War, Hitler had, like thousands of other young men, joined up to do his bit. As a despatch runner dodging shells and bullets in the trenches, he did more than many and deserved his decorations. Even so, there was something odd about Hitler. He never got drunk, never visited a prostitute. He always had his head in a book. He disliked Communists and he disliked Jews, but that was by no means unusual in wartime Germany. And as for his blindness, caused, he said, by a gas attack, that was psychosomatic – he was not blind at all.

The Jewish officer, Lieutenant Hugo Gutmann, had put Hitler forward for the Iron Cross and he was not the only superior who believed the corporal could be useful. Germany was falling apart at the end of 1918, not least Munich, where Hitler's regiment was based. It was taken over by the Communists under the journalist Kurt Eisner and soldiers like Hitler, bitter and disillusioned at being let down by their government in what was being referred to as 'the stab in the back' were bewildered and confused. Against the new Communist regime were a number of right-wing groups, collectively called the *Freikorps*. One of these was the SDAP, the not yet National Socialist Workers' Party. The very name 'Socialist' implied a confusion which also gave the group a wide appeal. At first there were several Communists among its members.

And one of the new faces that turned up at meetings in the Munich bierkellers was Adolf Hitler. There is little doubt that he was working for Mayr or someone else in the army's Intelligence unit. In other words, he was a spy. For the sake of verisimilitude, he had to join the NSDAP, which he did as party member 555. In later years, he would claim that his number was 7 – in other words, he had been a founder member – one of the many pieces of misinformation that the Nazis cultivated in the years ahead.

It was in those chaotic months of 1919-20 that Hitler discovered his skill for oration. Kurt Ludecke, who heard him, wrote, 'I forgot everything but the man. Clanking around, I saw that his magnetism was holding these thousands as one.'

Under the tutelage of Dietrich Eckart, poet and journalist who invented the much-hear battle-cry of these years – *'Deutschland Erwache!'* (Germany, awake!) – Hitler became the mob orator par excellence and slowly by surely replaced the railway worker Anton Drexler as head of the party. He embraced the Thule Society which promulgated Aryan racial supremacy. He designed the *hakencreuz*, the broken cross or swastika that had become the party's emblem. By July 1921, the Nazis had become national and if there was ever anything socialistic about their policies, that was phased out.

Eckhart died two years later, by which time Hitler was launching his abortive coup in Munich and writing *Mein Kampf*, the bible of the Nazi party. His last words were – 'Follow Hitler. He will dance, but it is I who have written the music ...'

From undercover agent to Fuhrer; it only took thirteen years. From Fuhrer to a petrol-soaked corpse in a bombed garden in Berlin; that took thirteen years too.

THE WAR OF THE WORLDS

!!

'Who would have believed that on 30 October 1938, millions of Americans were duped into believing that the Martians had landed and that New Yorkers were vapourised by ray guns.'

This is a paraphrase (sort of!) of the start of H.G. Wells' brilliant science fiction story which was dramatized by the actor Orson Welles on CBS radio on the date above.

The foaflore existed for years that American listeners really believed Wells'/Welles' fiction, assuming that it was a live-coverage broadcast. On 8 November 1938, Hitler referred to the panic that ensued as a classic example of the 'corrupt condition and decadent state of affairs in democracy'.

In 1930s America, as elsewhere, radio was a new kid on the block in terms of attention-grabbing media (rather as television is battling against YouTube, Tik Tok, Twitter and the rest today). Newspapers like the *New York Times*, anxious not to lose advertising revenue to radio claimed that 'terror by radio' was an example of the immorality and irresponsibility of the new outlet. Among the fake news stories that the papers ran were colossal traffic-jams bringing American cities to a standstill, mobs rioting in the streets and suicides happening all over the place. Bearing in mind the genuine hysteria from time to time in the United States, usually to do with race, nothing surprised the world any more; over 10,000 newspaper articles ran in the weeks after the show was aired. Such was the pull of all this that thousands who had not heard the play claimed that they had and remembered the ensuing panic too. CBS researchers phoned 5,000 households – only 2 per cent had actually heard it!

The play made Orson Welles' reputation and it did no harm to the bank balance of H.G. either. In fact, America need not have worried at all. The Welles' version is set in Princeton, but the 'real' Martian landing, as envisaged by Wells, happened in Woking, England. And to prove it, a statue of an alien 'grey' stands on the site today!

WENT THE DAY WELL?

!

Most of the war movies relating to 1939-45 were made in the 1950s and early '60s, starring the lantern-jawed British and American heart-throbs of the day. John Wayne often featured, even though he never saw an actual day's action in his life. Jack Hawkins, Anthony Steele, Richard Attenborough and John Mills provided the British muscle with a number of cheeky chappies like Harry Fowler and Victor Maddern to provide the light relief.

Went the Day Well? is different from all these, if only because it was made in 1942, when the war was at its height. From a short story by Graham Greene, directed by Alberto Cavalcanti, the film was produced at the Ealing Studios by Michael Balcon, perhaps Britain's most famous producer at the time. In a plotline often copied since, the fictional village of Bramley End (actually Turville in Buckinghamshire) is overrun by Wehrmacht troops in disguise. This is the start of a German invasion which was very much on the cards when Greene wrote the original story and it highlights the fear surrounding the existence of a fifth column spy network in the country. The actor Leslie Banks played the local squire in league with the Nazis and David Farrar was the handsome lead. The ever-reliable Mervyn Johns was the narrator, looking back on the events at Bramley End from the perspective of a war that was won (even though at the time, no one could have known the outcome). It was Thora Hird's first film and yes, of course Harry Fowler was in it!

The film's title comes from a poem written towards the end of the First World War by John Maxwell Edmonds –

> Went the day well?
> We died and never knew,
> But, well or ill,
> Freedom, we died for you.

Despite the fact that there is very little violence in it, it was included in *100 Greatest War Films* in 2005. Its black and white quirky nostalgia sets it apart from the more obvious gung-ho heroics of later movies and sums up superbly the hopes and sang-froid of a generation.

THE WHITE ROSE OF STALINGRAD

!

T he war in the east would be over quickly. Von Runstadt unleashed his blitzkrieg (lightning war) on the west with the overthrow of four countries in three month, Hitler could now turn his attention to his real goal – the subjugation of the Soviet Union. The Russians were genetically inferior *untermenschen* (sub-human), he believed and against the combined might of the Wehrmacht and the Luftwaffe, stood no chance. Operation Barbarossa, named after a Medieval emperor who had led the third crusade, was launched on 22 June 1941. Perhaps it was an unlucky code-name; Barbarossa never reached the Holy Land but drowned in a swollen river on his way to war.

Initially all went as planned. Stalin seems to have been blindsided by his former ally and was caught napping. In clash after clash, the massive Red Army fell back, exactly as earlier Russian armies had done in the First World War and against Napoleon in 1812. The problem was that the German fighting machine relied on speed and success – it was not equipped for a long, drawn-out struggle in which the Russian weather took its toll and petrol froze in fuel tanks. At Leningrad, Moscow and Stalingrad, the Red Army held on with a tenacity that was unexpected by anyone.

Women had fought in the Revolution of 1917, both for the Reds and the Whites, and by 1941 there were perhaps

800,000 of them serving in the army and 200,000 in air defence (see 'The Night Witches'). The Germans had their own Teutonic legends of the Valkyrie, terrible female spirits who swooped down onto battlefields to take the souls of the dead to a warrior-heaven called Valhalla. But they had never seen anyone like Lilya Litoyak. She signed up as a pilot although she had very little flying experience, refused to crop her hair as other Russian women did. She was punished for snazzing up her uniform with a fur collar but most party commissars, paid snoopers who insisted on slavish devotion to the party line, turned a blind eye.

Lilya's first known victory was over Erwin Meier, a Luftwaffe fighter pilot shot down by her over Stalingrad. He survived and was taken prisoner, but never believed that the petite blonde he had been introduced to, had actually brought him down. She was the first woman in history to kill in aerial warfare, and her plane, painted with a lily on the fuselage and with a cockpit full of flowers, assumed the same kind of totemic power of Manfred von Richthofen's red tin-plane in the First World War.

Her reputation grew as kill after kill was credited to her. In the British and American press, the lily morphed into a rose, hence the nickname and title of this section. By the age of 21 she was a squadron leader.

Lily flew her last mission on 1 August 1943. Her plane was shot down, but whether she died in the burning cockpit or was taken prisoner was unknown.

'WHO DO YOU THINK YOU ARE KIDDING, MR. HITLER?'

!!!

The Second World War was marked, among other things, by some spectacular photographs. Before it began, we have the British Prime Minister Neville Chamberlain holding up the worthless 'scrap of paper' on which Adolf Hitler promised peace in Europe. We have the dome of St Pauls Cathedral in London, still standing as the Blitz of 1940 rages all around it. We have British Tommies wading out to the 'little boats' that would rescue them at Dunkirk. We have the young men of the RAF's fighter command – Churchill's few – 'scrambling' to their Hurricanes as the air raid siren sounds. We have the American ships at Pearl Harbor, blazing and belching black smoke. We have terrified British and American troops about to leap out of their landing craft onto the Normandy beaches on D-Day. We have hundreds of parachutes floating like mushrooms over Holland in Operation Market Garden. We have the Stars and Stripes being lifted by battle-weary GIs on Iwo Jima. We have three utterly destroyed cities – Berlin, Hiroshima and Nagasaki.

Each photograph tells a poignant story of the bloodiest war in history. But there are some photographs that tell a vastly different tale. Expert Martin Dammann has collected hundreds of war photographs and has published them in a 2018 book, *Soldier Studies*: *Cross Dressing in Der Wehrmacht*. For years there were black propaganda stories of Nazis wearing women's clothing which were designed to blacken their reputations still further. Homosexuality was illegal across Europe in the 1940s and was a particular anathema to the Nazis who put people in concentration camps for it.

The truth was that pre-war Berlin was highly cosmopolitan, with a transexual elite personified by the characters in the musical *Cabaret*. The Nazi regime contrasted sharply with the decadence of Weimar and yet Damman's photographs are living proof that homosexuality, even sometimes in jest, was rife in the German armed forces.

WHOSE SIDE ARE YOU ON?

!

While most of us in the west have a clear idea of the broad brush-strokes of the Second World War, there are always little hidden corners which history has overlooked. One of those was the war in Finland.

From the Russian point of view, the Second World War was an opportunity to spread the word of Communism beyond the boundaries of the Soviet Union, and Finland, geographically so near, was an obvious example. One young man affected by this was Lauri Törni who despised communism and joined the Finish army to fight it. A determined and physically impressive soldier, he came to his superiors' attention at the bloody clashes at Lake Ladoga in the south of the country. The Red Army was vast and powerful but it had little experience of guerrilla warfare in heavy snow and across frozen lakes. The Finns fought them to a standstill, but inevitably had to agree an armistice when no help was forthcoming (despite being promised) from France or Britain. Soviet losses in this war were appalling.

By June 1941 Törni was wearing a different uniform. At the height of the Russo-Finnish war, operating deep behind enemy lines and causing havoc, there was a bounty of three million Finnish markka on his head. Now, he had joined the Waffen SS. Three years later, Finland and the Soviet Union had come to an agreement that any German forces still in the country must be demobilised and expelled.

By January 1945, Törni was in Germany being trained as a saboteur and found himself fighting against the Red Army near Schwerin. Here he surrendered to British troops and was marched to a POW camp at Lubeck a month after the war ended. Back in Finland, Törni tried to rejoin the family he had not seen for over two years but he was arrested in Helsinki and tried for treason for joining the German army. He was sentenced to six years in prison.

Having already escaped from the camp at Lubeck, Törni had something of a taste for it and he got out again before another re-arrest. In December 1948 he was pardoned by President Juho Paasikivi.

There can have been fewer spirits more restless than Lauri Törni. He went to Sweden and, under the alias of a Swedish seaman, took a ship bound for Venezuela. When the craft docked in the United States, Törni jumped it and became a political refugee in 'Finntown', New York's Finnish-American community in Brooklyn.

By 1954, Lauri Törni had become Larry Thorne of the United States Army, joining the Special Forces and becoming a captain by 1960. Three years later, he was fighting the communists again, this time in the form of the Vietcong in the grim jungles of Vietnam. He won a Bronze Star and no less than five Purple Hearts.

In 1965 Törni's luck ran out. The man who had fought in three armies, but all of them against the left, was in a CH-34 helicopter when the craft disappeared in smoke over Laos. It was not until 1999 that the wreckage was found and what was left of Törni's body was brought back to be buried with full military honours at Arlington National Cemetery. His arch-enemy, Russia's Soviet Union, had been buried twelve years earlier.

THE WIGWAM MURDER

!!

Criminologists call it 'the last of the classic cases' but if it remains relatively unknown today, it is because it was a crime that happened in wartime. As Graham Greene wrote in *The Ministry of Fear* in 1942, 'Nobody troubled about single deaths … in the middle of a massacre'.

The single death came to light on 7 October of that year, when a couple of marines on a routine march in woodland in Hankley Common on the Surrey-Sussex border stumbled on the decomposing body of a girl. Detailed forensic work and the discovery of personal items scattered nearby confirmed that her name was Joan Pearl Wolfe and she was a sixteen year old runaway.

The problem for the Surrey CID was that, not only was there a war on, with all police forces stretched to breaking point, but the murder scene was surrounded by army camps. Thousands of British and Canadians were in the area and any one of them – or more of them – could have killed Joan Wolfe.

As was customary in those days, the local police called in the homicide experience of Scotland Yard, in particular the lantern-jawed Chief Inspector Ted Greeno, who led the inquiry. House-to-house investigations and the full support of the military led to Joan's identity. She was what was still referred to in 1942 as a 'camp follower', a teenager tempted by the lure of young men in uniform. There had been several in Joan's young life, but the current 'squeeze' was August Sangret of the Regina Rifles of Saskatchewan.

Sangret was a Meti, a half-blood Cree native Canadian and French trapper from early colonial days. Strikingly good-looking and taciturn in the extreme, Sangret was grilled by Greeno for five days and produced the longest statement in British criminal history up to that point. He admitted that he knew Joan and they he risked punishment by nipping out from the camp to be with her in the 'wigwam' he built for them both in Hounsdown Wood, near a tank-training ground. Newspapers at the time and a number of ill-informed commentators since, have pictured the scene out of one of Edward Curtis's photographs of the 1880s – a plains 'Indian' in full war bonnet living in a buffalo-skin tepee. In fact, the Cree built their lodges of bent branches and leaves and August Sangret never wore anything except his Canadian khaki.

Sangret's story was that Joan had told him she was pregnant and they had fallen out about it, after which she disappeared and he spent some time trying to find her. The forensics of the case were carried out by Keith Simpson, the Home Office pathologist who concluded that the girl was first stabbed in the forehead with a pen-knife with a broken blade – 'like a parrot's beak'. She was then bludgeoned from behind with a birch branch which shattered her skull.

Sangret was arrested and put on trial at the Old Bailey in March 1943. The jury and the crowd gasped when Simpson produced Joan's skull to prove his point; it was the first time that such an exhibit was shown in court. Joan was Sangret's girl. She was pregnant which may have displeased him. They lived together on and off. The penknife with the peculiar blade was Sangret's. The jury found him guilty and he was sentenced to death by Mr Justice Macnaghten.

It all might have ended there, but today we would not be as certain as the jurors of 1943 over Sangret's guilt. It was Sangret's knife, but did he use it? The weapon passed through any number of hands while the case was being investigated. There were traces of blood on a blanket that Sangret owned, but it could not be tied to Joan Wolfe. She was not pregnant as she had claimed, so a potential motive disappeared. There were a number of other men in Joan's life who were not questioned once Sangret slotted into the frame.

He was hanged by Albert Pierrepoint who would go on to execute a number of Nazi leaders at Nuremberg three years later, at Wandsworth Prison. 'He lay there,' Molly LeFebure, Simpson's secretary remembered, 'muscular, well-built ... his handsome bronzed skin marked only by the imprint of the hangman's noose around his neck ...'

The judge had said during his summing up – 'there is no evidence that there ever was blood on this man'. The jury disagreed. Despite the dishonour surrounding his death, the Overseas Canada's Roll of Honour of 3 May 1943 includes his name – 'Royal Canadian Service Corps – Sangret, August, Pte. L27572'. As far as most of the world knows today, he died a soldier's death.

ZIGZAG

!

Whose side was he on? Spy fiction is full of examples of double, triple, quadruple agents, but Eddie Chapman was real. The best *actual* agents are unobtrusive, anonymous, careful (think George Smiley in the John le Carre novels). The least successful are the flash attention-seekers, the 007 wannabees who substitute violence, fast cars and beautiful girls for clever espionage.

What raises alarm bells about Chapman is that he was a career criminal and did nothing without serious payment. His handler in wartime Britain was John Masterman of the XX Committee, itself known as Double Cross, not just because of the Roman numerals but because it was specifically the Committee's job to 'turn' agents from their original masters. Masterman wrote in his memoirs that Chapman arrived from Jersey in December 1942, where he had been imprisoned for safe-blowing. Jersey of course had been occupied by the Wehrmacht and Chapman had offered his services to them in exchange for freedom. He was dropped by parachute near Ely, one of the very few enemy agents who was not interrogated and hanged as common criminals.

Chapman was charming and debonair, the arch conman, with a fund of useful information about enemy radio transmissions and military operations in the Nantes area of France. His task for the Germans was to sabotage the de Haviland works at Hatfield in Hertfordshire where they made Mosquito aircraft. He carried £1,000 in cash and explosives and had been promised £15,000 (a vast sum) to pull the bombing off.

Masterman took a chance. He 'turned' Chapman (although the jury is still out as to how much of that was required), gave him the codename Zigzag and faked a successful attack on the Hatfield factory. The Germans bought it, gleefully viewing the photos of 'bomb damage' on 29 January 1943 and taking press reports as genuine.

With British SIS connivance, Chapman got a job as steward on the merchantman *City of Lancaster* and when it reached Lisbon in neutral Portugal, he contacted the Germans and was secretly hailed as a hero. He had ambitious plans, which he outlined to Masterman, to set up a Fifth Column in France and even assassinate Hitler as a one-man killing machine. The idea was taken up by Geoffrey Household in this short story *Rogue Male*, later televised and starring Peter O'Toole. In the event, Masterman turned him down.

Little was heard of Zigzag until 1944 when news reached Masterman of someone in neutral Oslo speaking bad German in a loud voice. He had two gold teeth, awful clothes and lived on a private yacht. He also had, although few people knew it, an Iron cross given to him by a grateful nation! In June of that year, he parachuted near Cambridge with two wireless sets and £6,000 spending money. He had been fully accepted by the Nazi authorities in Nantes and his task this time was to report on the damage caused by V1 and V2 missiles and the organization and whereabouts of US airbases. He reported that Berlin looked like the 'ruins of Pompeii' and that morale in the Germany Kreigsmarine (Navy) was particularly low.

The problem was that by now, Chapman had let his successful double life go to his head. He began to talk about his cases and that, to Masterman at least, was the kiss of death. He was dropped from all future operations.

After the war, it could all come out – or at least, Chapman's version of it. In 1954, he wrote an autobiography, *The Eddie Chapman Story*, but whether he was actually Zigzag, as the British knew him, or Fritzchen, his German codename, will probably never be known.

KILROY
WAS
HERE

Other titles by BLKDOG Publishing for your consideration:

Maxwell's Summer
By M. J. Trow

Peter Maxwell is looking forward to a nice quiet summer, with perhaps a little light gardening if necessary – as long as the plants don't grow over the door and trap them all inside, it won't be necessary. But, as so often in Maxwell's life, Mrs Troubridge happens and a day out for her and her special friend, Mrs Getty, takes Maxwell and Nolan to Haledown House and from there into a web of intrigue and death.

Maxwell's Summer turns out to be nothing like he planned. As resident conversationalist at a stately home, with riding lessons on the side for Nolan and free dinners when she wants them for Jacquie, Mad Max Maxwell could be forgiven for expecting a pretty easy time of it – with a nice fat cheque thrown in. But murders soon cross his path – almost literally – and with his own life in danger, will he even make it to the dreaded A Level Results Day?

Closing Time
By Various Authors

They say a stranger is just someone you haven't met yet.

But chance works in mysterious ways.

Several strangers end up at *The Whistler* on Saturday night, a popular pub in London's vibrant and cosmopolitan Soho district.

These strangers will find, when the clock strikes 22:22, that fate and circumstance has linked and intertwined them in ways they could never have imagined.

Welcome to *The Whistler*, we hope you enjoy your stay.

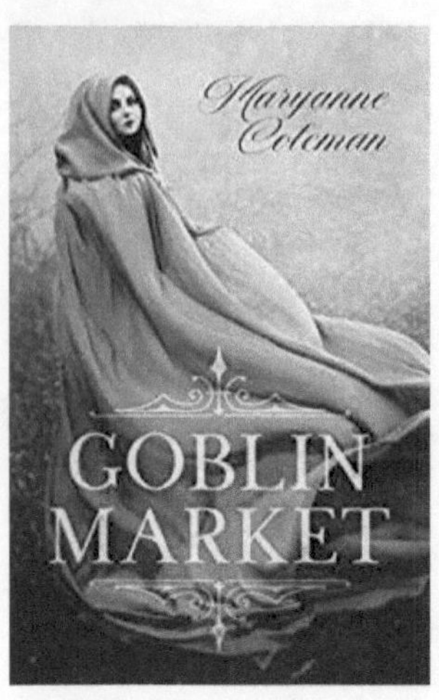

Goblin Market
By Maryanne Coleman

Have you ever wondered what happened to the faeries you used to believe in? They lived at the bottom of the garden and left rings in the grass and sparkling glamour in the air to remind you where they were. But that was then – now you might find them in places you might not think to look. They might be stacking shelves, delivering milk or weighing babies at the clinic. Open your eyes and keep your wits about you and you might see them.

But no one is looking any more and that is hard for a Faerie Queen to bear and Titania has had enough. When Titania stamps her foot, everyone in Faerieland jumps; publicity is what they need. Television, magazines. But that sort of thing is much more the remit of the bad boys of the Unseelie Court, the ones who weave a new kind of magic; the World Wide Web. Here is Puck re-learning how to fly; Leanne the agent who really is a vampire; Oberon's Boys playing cards behind the wainscoting; Black Annis, the bag-lady from Hainault, all gathered in a Restoration comedy that is strictly twenty-first century.

Prester John: Africa's Lost King
By Richard Denham

He sits on his jewelled throne on the Horn of Africa in the maps of the sixteenth century. He can see his whole empire reflected in a mirror outside his palace. He carries three crosses into battle and each cross is guarded by one hundred thousand men. He was with St Thomas in the third century when he set up a Christian church in India. He came like a thunderbolt out of the far East eight centuries later, to rescue the crusaders clinging on to Jerusalem. And he was still there when Portuguese explorers went looking for him in the fifteenth century.

He went by different names. The priest who was also a king was Ong Khan; he was Genghis Khan; he was Lebna Dengel. Above all, he was a Christian king who ruled a vast empire full of magical wonders: men with faces in their chests; men with huge, backward-facing feet; rivers and seas made of sand. His lands lay next to the earthly Paradise which had once been the Garden of Eden. He wrote letters to popes and princes. He promised salvation and hope to generations.

But it was noticeable that as men looked outward, exploring more of the natural world; as science replaced superstition and the age of miracles faded, Prester John was always elsewhere. He was beyond the Mountains of the Moon, at the edge of the earth, near the mouth of Hell.

Was he real? Did he ever exist? This book will take you on a journey of a lifetime, to worlds that might have been, but never were. It will take you, if you are brave enough, into the world of Prester John.

Fade
By Bethan White

There is nothing extraordinary about Chris Rowan. Each day he wakes to the same faces, has the same breakfast, the same commute, the same sort of homes he tries to rent out to unsuspecting tenants.

There is nothing extraordinary about Chris Rowan. That is apart from the black dog that haunts his nightmares and an unexpected encounter with a long forgotten demon from his past. A nudge that will send Chris on his own downward spiral, from which there may be no escape.

There is nothing extraordinary about Chris Rowan...

The Children's Crusade
By M. J. Trow

In the summer of 1212, 30,000 children from towns and villages all over France and Germany left their homes and families and began a crusade. Their aim; to retake Jerusalem, the holiest city in the world, for God and for Christ. They carried crosses and they believed, because the Bible told them so, that they could cross the sea like Moses. The walls of Jerusalem would fall, like Jericho's did for Joshua.

It was the age of miracles – anything was possible. Kings ignored the Children; so did popes and bishops. The handful of Church chroniclers who wrote about them were usually disparaging. They were delusional, they were inspired not by God, but the Devil. Their crusade was doomed from the start.

None of them reached Outremer, the Holy Land. They turned back, exhausted. Some fell ill on the way; others died. Others still were probably sold into slavery to the Saracens – the very Muslims who had taken Jerusalem in the first place.

We only know of three of them by name – Stephen, Nicholas and Otto. One of them was a shepherd, another a ploughboy, the third a scholar. The oldest was probably fourteen. Today, in a world where nobody believes in miracles, the Children of 1212 have almost been forgotten.

Almost… but not quite…

The poet Robert Browning caught the mood in his haunting poem, *The Pied Piper of Hamelin*, bringing to later readers the sad image of a lost generation, wandering a road to who knew where.

www.blkdogpublishing.com